FLOATER

Books by Calvin Trillin

Alice, Let's Eat
Runestruck
American Fried
U.S. Journal
Barnett Frummer Is an Unbloomed Flower
An Education in Georgia

Floater

Calvin Trillin

Ticknor & Fields

NEW HAVEN AND NEW YORK

Design: Sally Harris/Summer Hill Books

Library of Congress Cataloging in Publication Data

Trillin, Calvin.
  Floater.
    I. Title.
PZ4.T83Fl [PS3570.R5] 813'.54   80-17337
ISBN 0-89919-017-0

Printed in the United States of America

s   10   9   8   7   6   5   4   3

TO MY SISTER, SUKEY FOX

CLAIMER

The character of Andy Wolferman is based on
John Gregory Dunne, though it tends to flatter.
The other characters are fictional.

Sunday night

1 As the limousine pulled up to the visitors' gate of the White House, both of the men in the back seat began lighting their pipes. A White House policeman walked out of the guard booth and approached the driver's window, carrying a clipboard. "Mr. Fenton and Mr. Holbrook to see the President," the driver of the limousine said. The policeman referred to his clipboard, then looked carefully at the two men in the back seat. Woodrow Fenton, who was puffing contentedly on his pipe, nodded at the policeman—the sort of amiable, satisfied nod that a pastor might use to acknowledge the banquet chairman's thanks for having just delivered the invocation. Ralph Holbrook lit his sixth match and puffed furiously, trying to coerce the pipe into burning smoothly—his lips making loud popping noises as they parted with each puff. He had only been smoking a pipe for six weeks. It was said around the magazine that he had taken up pipe smoking simply because Woody Fenton smoked a pipe, just as he had moved to Mamaroneck because Woody Fenton lived in Mamaroneck, but that was, in fact, not the case. He had taken up pipe smoking because he had been given reason to believe

that he would be invited to accompany Woody Fenton to the White House if the President called Fenton in for a private briefing. Holbrook was hoping to come away with some White House matchbooks, and he needed a natural way to display them.

The White House policeman checked their names off on his clipboard, initialed two large cardboard passes, punched the passes into a time clock that was attached to the outside of the guard booth, and gave each of them a pass. Then he nodded to the driver—a nod that also signaled someone in the booth to push a button, causing the gate in front of them to unlock itself with a metallic clank and slowly swing open. The limousine proceeded through the gate. Woody Fenton turned toward Holbrook and, without taking his pipe out of his mouth, said, "Golly!"

Holbrook smiled and nodded. He was known for his quick smile—a tight, cheerless baring of the teeth that always ended as abruptly as it had begun. Behind his back, a number of writers on the magazine referred to him as Syracuse Smiley. He always smiled while announcing something unpleasant—say, informing a writer who had at last found happiness doing the Entertainment Arts section while living the high life in New York that an opening in the Detroit bureau presented a great opportunity to exploit his real talents.

On the other hand, a silent smile was generally considered as good a response as any to one of Woody Fenton's gollies. Fenton always seemed to be saying golly, although he also let out a breathless "Gosh!" now and then, and occasionally said "Gee whiz!" Once, a student of modern dance who was working temporarily as a copy boy claimed to have heard Fenton respond to one of the minor catastrophes that accompanied the magazine's closing night once a week by shouting "Jumping Jehoshaphat!" but the claim had never been independently verified. All of the writers on the magazine were accustomed to receiving from the managing editor's office newspaper clippings pinned to a piece of copy paper upon which was written a single "Golly!" or "Gee!" Despite several thousand hours of discussion on the subject by writers and researchers and even senior editors, nobody had ever devised a satisfactory explanation for why an educated man in his early sixties, a man sophisticated enough to preside over a national newsmagazine, should use the folksy expletive as his principal device for communication. Nor had anyone devised a satisfactory explanation for precisely what the folksy expletives were meant to communicate. What exactly did a scrawled "Golly!" next to a *New York Times* item on home air conditioning mean? There was general agreement that Fenton's gollies were not meant ironically. An affable man, with a ruddy complexion and watery blue eyes and short gray hair, Woody Fenton had what one of his writers, Andrew Wolferman, had called "a face so open that one is tempted to walk through it."

"Heck of an operation they've got," Fenton went on, perhaps explaining the golly. Fenton often commented with wonder on such modern commonplaces as automatically opening gates or electronic scoreboards. Some people thought such remarks reflected the broad curiosity that had once made Woody Fenton a competent newspaper reporter; other people thought it reflected the fact that he had nothing else on his mind.

At the side entrance of the White House, they were

met by a polite young man who was wearing the proudly harried look often seen at the magazine on the faces of people known as "crisis hounds"—editors who preferred to pause for a three-hour supper on the evening the magazine was supposed to go to press and then do their final editing in the hours after midnight, slurping coffee and shouting emergency instructions to researchers and staving off frantic telephone calls from the printers. The young man escorted them to a small sitting room. He said that the President would be with them as soon as possible, and then he left. Fenton and Holbrook both settled into armchairs. Holbrook's pipe had gone out, and he started working at it again. For five minutes they sat without speaking. "Gee," Fenton finally said—referring to the wait, perhaps, or to the portrait over the fireplace of an unfamiliar-looking man who presumably might once have been President, or to the thick Persian rug, or to the self-opening gate once again. A steward—a black man in his fifties, wearing a stiff white jacket—came in and asked them if they would care for a drink. They both ordered Perrier water with a twist. The steward had hardly left the room when the same polite young man who had greeted them returned.

"Terribly sorry," he said. "The President's had to leave. The First Lady's at Camp David, and she's feeling quite ill. Nothing serious—just intestinal flu or something. But she's really feeling rotten, so the President's decided he'd better go down to see her before taking the Midwest swing in the morning. So he's off in the chopper. Probably there in six or seven minutes from now. I'm awfully sorry—you coming all the way down here, and all. If it's all right with you, we can reschedule for early Thursday morning, after he gets back from Chicago."

Fenton and Holbrook left the room with the young man and walked toward the side door, where the limousine was waiting. "Golly!" Fenton said, as soon as they had settled back into the limousine. Holbrook smiled quickly. "Gee," Fenton went on. "Amazing—what they can do in those choppers."

Holbrook wondered if the steward would have brought White House matchbooks with the drinks.

Monday

Fred Becker began making out a proposed story list for the Lifestyle section—shuffling through the suggestions from the bureaus, pausing for a couple of minutes to wonder about a Teletyped message from the Los Angeles bureau proposing a story on "the hot new fashion rage of two-thirds stockings." Did that mean two-thirds of the way up the leg or two-thirds of the way to the knee? Could it possibly mean the remaining two-thirds of what had been a conventional stocking, with patches of bare leg indicating that the material from the other third had been donated to Sioux militants or to a fund for the preservation of the blue whale? The suggestion from Los Angeles gave no hint of what a two-thirds stocking actually was, and Becker, concluding that it didn't make much difference, added two-thirds stockings to the list. He glanced at his watch. He had an hour before he had to present the proposed list at the Lifestyle story conference. He turned to a wire from the Phoenix stringer suggesting that Lifestyle do a story on a study showing the danger of baton-twirling during the last trimester of pregnancy.

"Medicine," he mumbled aloud, as he tossed the wire into the wastebasket. "Maybe Sports."

"Don't get too settled," he heard from the door. "Doc's looking a bit queasy this morning."

Becker looked up to see Pam Robinson, the Medicine researcher, standing in the doorway. "Doesn't Doc usually feel kind of sick on Mondays?" he asked.

"Always," Pam said. Doc Kennedy, the regular Medicine writer, often found himself with the symptoms of the diseases he wrote about, in the way that medical students sometimes develop the symptoms of the diseases they study. Kennedy was usually able to carry on, but sometimes, doubled over with what seemed to be colitis or a deteriorating disc or the effects of an intestinal bypass operation, he would have to be helped into a taxi by Pam Robinson and sent home for the rest of the week. Then Becker was usually called in to write whatever part of the section Kennedy, in his pain, had been unable to get to. Becker was what the magazine called a floater. He moved from section to section—acquiring an authoritative medical tone whenever Doc Kennedy was struck down by the symptoms of some rare ailment, becoming instantly knowledgeable in commercial matters when one of the Business writers was off tending his investments, plugging away at Religion while the regular Religion writer, Rob Rowan, was off for what eventually began to seem like eternity.

Becker didn't mind Medicine, except when the stories dealt with innards of one sort or another. He sometimes suspected that Doc Kennedy might share his bias: Kennedy's attacks of what seemed to be cholera or kwashiorkor often coincided with the Medicine section's scheduling of some gruesome study of colon repair techniques. "What's the list look like?" Becker asked Pam.

She pursed her lips and shook her head. "Strictly kishkes," she said. "A long wrap-up on the pancreas. If you have any choice, avoid it like the plague."

"Is that what Doc thinks he has today—the plague?"

"No, he hasn't had the plague since last fall," Pam said. "What he seems to have today are all of the classic symptoms of bilharzia."

"Jesus Christ! What's bilharzia?"

"A parasitic disease carried in the feces of a certain kind of snail," Pam said. "A lot of Africans have it chronically from contact with streams or ponds where the snails live. Very debilitating. Doc wrote about it last week, poor thing."

"I don't suppose there's a cure."

"There is, but it involves a series of shots in the stomach with a very long needle," Pam said. "I don't think you want to hear the details."

"You're right, you're right," Becker said, turning his head away and holding out his hand like a traffic cop to stop the description. Pam left, and Becker went back to the Lifestyle list, picking up a suggestion from the Dallas bureau about a new rage for holding debutante cotillions on horseback. Shouldn't that be Sports? He went on to the second paragraph, which revealed that it was not the riders but the horses that were coming out. Definitely Sports. He tossed the suggestion into his wastebasket, hoping that other copies of it were getting the same treatment. The other five or six people who would be at the Lifestyle story conference had access to the same Teletype copies and

Xeroxed newspaper clippings that he was reading, but the writer of a section was traditionally responsible for serving up proposed stories for the approval or disapproval of the senior editor in charge. The response was never predictable in Lifestyle, since it was one of the sections within the purview of a senior editor named Pete Smithers, who, according to a theory widespread among writers and researchers, had as his only conceivable qualification for the job a unique and rather interesting way of leaning back in his desk chair. Smithers was almost always found leaning back from his desk at a drastic angle—his legs absolutely straight, his heels hooked precariously on the edge of his desk, and his feet spread at the toes to form a perfect V-shaped frame through which he regarded the writer standing before him, like a man sighting very carefully through a large gunsight.

"That son of a bitch knows how to put his feet on the desk," someone would always say, when the subject of Pete Smithers came up in a gathering of writers.

"He could give lessons in it."

"You can't take that away from old Pete. He's the master all right—staring up at you through his Bass Weejuns with those beady little eyes."

"I hear Holbrook tried it once and fell on his ass."

"You lookin' for a guy who can lean back and put his feet on the desk, Pete Smithers is your man."

Becker put the pile of suggestions and clippings aside and walked to the window. He looked down at the streets of midtown Manhattan, twenty stories below. On Fifth Avenue, just within his sight, a street peddler was arranging a display of leather handbags that he would sell to the lunchtime crowd with the unspoken implication that they were stolen and therefore cheap—although, Becker knew from a story he had once done in Business, they had almost certainly been purchased quite legally from a Sephardic discounter in Queens. Becker was having trouble concentrating on the Lifestyle story list. The story that kept going through his mind had nothing to do with the Lifestyle section. It was a story he had been told in Washington the night before by Leonard Wentzell—a story about the President's wife.

3 "The President's wife!" Becker had said.

Wentzell brought one pudgy finger to his lips as if to say "shhh"—which should have been impossible for him to say, since his mouth was stuffed with potato chips. He glanced around the bar to see if anybody had overheard, although there was nobody near them. It was Sunday evening, and the place was almost deserted. They were in a dark, nondescript bar near Capitol Hill—the sort of place, Becker had always imagined, a congressman might come to with his secretary after work in the hope of softening her up enough with a few martinis to lure her back to the office for what he could later describe to his wife as "constituent servicing," and the sort of place a secretary might come to with a congressman in the hope of downing enough hors d'oeuvres to be able to make do without dinner. Becker had envisioned similar bars once while doing a Behavior section story on a study indicating that people drinking in bars were at their most despondent not just before closing, as had previously been assumed, but during a time of day known widely in cocktail lounges and bars as Happy Hour. Following Wentzell's gaze around the bar, Becker was reminded how much he hated Washington, where he had once spent two or three months as a junior member of the magazine's bureau. He glanced at his watch to see if he could possibly make the seven o'clock shuttle back to New York, although he knew perfectly well that he could never get away without what Wentzell always insisted on calling "a bit of a pub crawl."

"Did you say the President's wife?" Becker said, in a softer voice, leaning across the table toward Wentzell.

Wentzell closed his eyes and nodded very slowly. Becker recognized the gesture as Wentzell's most knowing nod. He had seen it dozens of times—the first time, as best he could remember, in 1952, when they were both six, and Wentzell nodded knowingly after assuring him that Koreans, like Japanese, did indeed have yellow blood. It was the same nod Wentzell had used several years later, while assuring Fred and three other boys on the block that researchers at the University of Nebraska were attempting to harness the human fart for powering mass transit. Becker couldn't recall ever having been with Wentzell without seeing the knowing nod at least once, usually in answer to a spoken or implied "really?" When Becker had last been in Washington—drinking with Wentzell at the same bar, six months before—they both happened to be watching the slow saunter of the waitress as she left their table to get them another round of drinks. "Ah, a flat butt," Wentzell had said. "The curse of the French Huguenot."

"A flat butt is an ethnic characteristic of French Huguenots?" Becker had said, before he could stop himself.

Knowing nod.

Apparently, Wentzell's eyes had not been all the way

closed when he indicated that it was indeed the President's wife he was talking about: while he was still nodding, he reached out an arm to stop a waitress who was passing the table, handed her the empty potato chip bowl, and said, "You wanna do it again, honey?"

Becker wondered whether it was possible to pretend not to know somebody you were sitting at a table for two with in an otherwise deserted bar. Wentzell was poking around the refilled potato chip bowl—guided, presumably, by his theory, often expressed to Becker, that particularly crisp potato chips are beneficial to the teeth and gums. He looked up at Becker with what was undoubtedly meant to be a conspiratorial grin—although Wentzell looked so conspiratorial to begin with that there was hardly any way to intensify the effect. Wentzell had not lost any weight since Becker's previous trip to Washington. He still seemed to be wearing clothes that belonged to someone who was not only a size or two smaller but also a completely different shape. Wentzell had smooth, dark skin and jet black hair, giving him a sort of Levantine look—like a man, Becker always thought, who made his living selling false identification papers in Istanbul. In high school—where nearly everybody, including Fred Becker, looked like the obvious result of nurturing Northern European genes in the Upper Midwest—Wentzell had been known as the Rug Merchant.

Becker knew that Wentzell came from completely nonexotic Midwestern stock—that his father, Claude Wentzell, the grandson of German and Swedish immigrants who had come to the Dakotas to homestead, was still a Pontiac dealer in Omaha—but Wentzell himself occasionally seemed to forget. Once, while Becker was serving his sentence in the Washington bureau, a newspaper reporter he met at a Department of Commerce press conference—a press conference that had been called, as far as Becker could make out, mainly to demonstrate that the commerce secretary had at his command an even larger store of impenetrable economic jargon than the secretary of the treasury did—told him about having met Wentzell. Before Becker could say that he had known Wentzell for years—having long ago decided that both "old childhood friend" and "old childhood acquaintance" were inappropriate descriptions, he occasionally found himself referring to Wentzell as "an old childhood phenomenon of mine"—the newspaper reporter said, "Really interesting background."

Becker had nodded, although he couldn't see anything really interesting about being the son of a Pontiac dealer in Omaha.

"That really must have been something—the only Lebanese family in a Mexican serape-weaving village," the newspaper reporter said. Becker shouldn't have been surprised. He had been present at a long, sodden party in Chevy Chase when Wentzell, without having said so in so many words, had left the impression that he was an Egyptian-born agent of the Israeli intelligence service. More than once, Becker had heard Wentzell discuss the burdens of being the son of a Greek oil-tanker billionaire or mention, in a conversation sprinkled with Yiddish words, the bizarre chain of events that resulted in a Rumanian gypsy boy's having been raised by an Orthodox Jewish merchant-seaman.

"What was the town in Mexico you told that reporter from Baltimore you were from?" he asked Wentzell, who was still poking around among the potato chips.

"Shmata Grande, Jalisco," Wentzell said.

"Shmata Grande," Becker repeated, shaking his head in amazement. "He believed Shmata Grande. Some reporter."

"Shmata Grande, Jalisco," Wentzell said. "I thought mentioning the province added a touch of verisimilitude."

"But what was the point of it—even with verisimilitude?"

"Cover, Freddy," Wentzell said. "It's all a matter of cover."

Becker nodded. Wentzell often talked like a CIA operative. He often made cryptic references to "some work I'm doing for the government" or "a little job I've been asked to take on." When, on visits home, Becker discussed the matter with old high-school classmates, they always agreed that Wentzell could not possibly be in the CIA. "If the Merchant was in the CIA, the Commies would control the whole world," Sonny Milledge, who had become a wealthy hamburger franchiser in Omaha, always said. "Why, they'd have the grain exchange. The whole works." That left the question of just what Wentzell did for a living. Becker had no idea, never having got beyond vague references to "a special project" or "one or two things here and there."

Becker stirred his drink. Wentzell discovered two or three more potato chips that met his qualifications and began chewing them carefully. Finally, Becker said, "The President of the United States?"

"What?"

"The President of the United States?" Becker repeated. "The president's wife you're talking about is the wife of the President of the United States?"

Wentzell looked at him for a while. "Freddy," he said.

"Pal of my youth. Buddy. Putz. Of course the President of the United States! Was it your impression that I was talking about the president of the United Way Campaign of Wahoo, Nebraska? The President of the United States is the president I'm talking about. More to the point—his wife. The First Lady. Planter of maples and sycamores. Protector of the lame and the loony. Beautifier of double lanes."

Wentzell fell silent, looking almost hurt—at least to the extent that, say, a Moroccan dealer in pornographic postcards can look hurt—at having been suspected of prying into the private life of someone of no importance. "Now that I think of it," he said, "what happened to that other dynamite story I gave you?"

"What other dynamite story?"

"When you were in Lifestyle, or whatever it is," Wentzell said. "Are you still in Lifestyle? Or Religion?"

"I'm in Lifestyle again," Becker said. "I got sprung from Religion a long time ago."

"You're still cruising?"

"Floating."

"So floating. Did the Religion writer turn out to have Communion Wafer Spotted Fever like I said?"

"We're not sure," Becker said. "He may have had a nervous breakdown or he may have had a religious experience or he may have had Communion Wafer Spotted Fever. What other dynamite story are you talking about?"

"The Disneyland story," Wentzell said. "Christ, that should have made your career at that meshuggeneh magazine."

"I couldn't seem to interest them in that one," Becker said. The Disneyland story had been a characteristic Wentzell tip. Glancing around conspiratorially in some other dark and nondescript bar near Capitol Hill, Wentzell had informed Becker that, according to an absolutely reliable source, the cheerful, clean-cut American boys who ran the jungle cruise at Disneyland occasionally shouted out numbers that everybody assumed to be concerned with boat capacity and crowd control but that actually were coded communications about the approach of any attractive female who was not wearing a bra. Becker had nodded, waiting for Wentzell to get to the story, but that, as it turned out, was the story. It was, at the very most, a four-line footnote to a Disneyland story; Wentzell spoke as if he expected to see it on the cover. "No sense of perspective is another reason the Rug Merchant could never be in the CIA," Sonny Milledge sometimes said. "He might get all excited and have someone assassinated for mispronouncing the President's name or something."

"That putz Fenton wouldn't know a story if it bit him on the ass," Wentzell was saying. "No news sense."

"Leonard," Becker said. "Let me get this straight. You're telling me that the President's wife—"

"Right," Wentzell said, nodding his knowing nod. "Addition on the way. Dividend in the mail. Biscuit in the oven. All that. I'm telling you that the President of the United States—the Commander in Chief, the Leader of the Free World—has knocked her up. And you, at this moment, know it before he does."

4 Becker made the nine o'clock shuttle on the run. There were only middle seats left. He plopped down between two large men, both of whom seemed to have come from an even longer pub crawl than the one he had endured with Wentzell. It was hot in the plane. Becker was feeling the effect of the drinks he had downed in the three bars Wentzell had managed to drag him to before he dashed for the airport. Although the plane hadn't left the ground, the man on his right had already nodded off to sleep and was beginning to snore. Becker started leafing through the Eastern Airlines magazine, reading with his elbows pressed into his stomach, but he was thinking about the President's wife.

There would, he acknowledged, be interesting implications if the First Lady really was pregnant. On the other hand, there would be interesting implications if Koreans and Japanese really had yellow blood. Wentzell had not, after all, spent his childhood peddling Mexican serapes to gringos in Shmata Grande, Jalisco. As it happened, though, Becker knew that the clean-cut youths who ran the jungle cruise at Disneyland really did pass the time by shouting out coded numbers that rated the breasts of approaching women. By chance, one of the copy boys at the magazine had been a ticket-taker at the jungle cruise one summer and was astonished to find that Becker knew the code (ten-nineteen for "unusually large," eight followed by a number from one to ten for "essential bounciness," etc.). It was hardly the sort of information that would make a news-magazine story—even though Becker himself had once, while substituting in Medicine during Doc Kennedy's attack of sympathetic hammertoes, written a story about a breast-rating system perfected by a Beverly Hills plastic surgeon who was known as "Breast-Lifter to the Stars"—but, still, it was at least true. Over the years, Wentzell had spoken the truth a number of times—usually out of the corner of his mouth, in a conspirational whisper. It could be that the President's wife was, in fact, with child.

"It does put him in a rather awkward position," Wentzell had said while they were at Micawber's, a claustrophobic saloon in Georgetown that seemed to be decorated in some warped vision of a nineteenth-century English railroad car—red plush seats and heavy drapes and a slight whiff of the second-class compartment. "He's fifty-four years old, pal of my youth. His other children are grown—grown into useless fathead layabouts, it's true, but still grown. He plans on having one more term and then retiring to write his memoirs in three volumes and acting like an elder statesman, right? Isn't that the way you figure it?"

"I suppose so," Becker said. Becker rarely wrote in the National News section, being a specialist in what was known as "the back of the book," and as a private citizen he did not have even the ordinary newspaper reader's interest in keeping up with what his high-school teacher always called Current Events. During his occasional stints in National News, he had found that in ten or fifteen minutes with the library file and the news clippings on, say, the gun lobby or Southern Republicanism or health insurance legislation, he could learn enough to adopt the confident style favored by the magazine. Most of the people at the magazine who specialized in the news that came out of Washington were bored by government but fascinated by politics; Becker was bored by both. When he was thirteen and a baseball zealot, his sister had ridiculed his interest in baseball games by saying, "They're all the same except for the score." At the time, the remark had seemed to him symbolic of her deep, feminine ignorance of what was truly important in life, but he later decided she had aptly described not only baseball games but also political campaigns. He found international affairs even more repetitious. Whenever he floated into the Foreign Affairs section, he always seemed to be writing a story he had written two or three times before, usually about Cyprus. For a while, he considered the possibility that the Greeks and Turks on Cyprus had some way of knowing when he was going to be assigned to Foreign Affairs. All over the island people would say, "He's there! He's there!" in Greek or Turkish, a signal for everyone to haul out the bombs and Bren guns for yet another chapter of the dreary conflict—absolutely indistinguishable from the chapter he had dealt with a year before.

"So who wants to be an elder statesman with a four-year-old brat on your hands?" Wentzell had continued. "Even more important, it's obvious that the First Lady preferred trees to children in the first place. I'm not saying I blame her of course, considering those arguments for zero population growth she already raised. But that's not the point, Frederic. The point is this: what does a lady a bit long in the tooth, looking forward to playing out the tea-time of her years on the golf course and the beautification circuit do when she's got what they call an unwanted pregnancy?"

Becker started to say "abortion," but as he formed the first syllable Wentzell again raised his finger to his lips as a signal that they could be overheard. Then he offered a short version of the knowing nod.

"Right, right," he said, practically in a whisper. "But there are a few tiny little political problems in this case. In the first place, as far as anybody knows, no President's wife has ever had an abortion while the knocker-upper was in office, right? Not even any presidential candidate's wife. Unheard of. Not known. Also, this particular President, sanctimonious shmuck that he is, has publicly said, in his never-ending efforts to get all the votes on both sides of every issue, that he wouldn't be for a constitutional amendment to ban abortion because it has to be a matter of individual choice, but that the individual choice that would be made by him and his sanctimonious little wife would be against it, because of their deeply felt religious mishegos and all that. What would happen, then, if, after all that, wifey set a White House record for most abortions while in office? Why, the right-to-life loonies would have him for breakfast. One can hardly calculate the effect on the election campaign, world peace, and his book advance."

It all made sense, Becker reflected as the shuttle finally began to rattle down the runway—causing the head of the fat man on his right to come to rest on his shoulder. Even if the President hadn't taken his essentially two-faced stand on abortion, the First Lady's having an abortion would be politically tricky. Under the circumstances, it would be disastrous. But why was Wentzell making this case to Fred Becker, back-of-the-book floater?

The question had come up while he and Wentzell were drinking in O'Brian's, an oppressively Irish bar near the White House—only blocks away from the (perhaps) impregnated subject of their discussion, unless she happened to be off somewhere dedicating a grove of pine trees.

"Leonard," Becker had said, trying to get Wentzell's attention away from the burnt cheeseburger he was attacking. "Leonard, why are you telling me all of this?"

Wentzell looked up from the cheeseburger. He looked genuinely surprised—but Becker had once seen him look genuinely surprised when a young woman he had been talking to in a bar all evening told him that she was not absolutely certain that she believed he was the son of the pretender to the throne of Albania. Wentzell put down his cheeseburger and licked his fingers. "Frederic," he said. "I'm surprised at you. Why am I telling you all of this? Because, pal of my youth, you are the pal of my youth. Because you saved me from the giant bully Rick Bengstrom by throwing a football at his private parts. Because you did not betray me in sixth grade when Miss McCandless asked who had put the harmless little water snake in the girls' loo. Because your triumphs are my triumphs. This is the story of the century, Freddy. Should I give it to a stranger? And Freddy—" Wentzell leaned over the table and signaled Becker to come closer so he could speak in a whisper, although they were the only people in O'Brian's except for a bartender—a large bearded man who was alternately reading silently and speaking softly lines of Brendan Behan poetry, apparently memorizing it for use on a late Saturday night Irish drinking crowd. "Freddy," Wentzell continued. "Listen. This one is true. I have a confession to make. I don't mind telling you now—that other story I gave you, about the boob-watching in Disneyland. That one I made up. I hated to tell you something that wasn't true, but it was part of a little project I was working on for some people. I can't go into it now." He winked conspiratorially and went back to his cheeseburger.

On the shuttle, Becker tried to edge away from the sleeping man far enough to get out his wallet. The stewardess was making her way slowly down the aisle, collecting fares. What if the Rug Merchant was telling the truth? It wasn't the story of the century, but it was a story. What use was it to a back-of-the-book floater? Fred Becker was not even exactly a reporter. He wrote his stories from the reports filed by correspondents in the field and from what the researcher found in the library and from what he managed to lift from the daily newspapers. What could be his reward for bringing in the story of the First Lady's pregnancy? Would the management be so impressed with his skills as an investigative reporter that it would impose on him an even longer sentence in the Washington bureau? Would his obvious grasp of the Washington scene earn him a permanent assignment in National News? He hated National News. Once, when Ralph Holbrook, flashing the smile that could only mean dismal tidings for the person smiled upon, told him that he was being rewarded for his skill and willingness as a floater with a fixed slot in National News, Becker had taken the unusual step of going over Holbrook's head to Woody Fenton to appeal the decision. (Fenton's response to Becker's entreaty that he be allowed to remain a floater had been, "Gee, sure, Fred.") It was possible, Becker realized, that for all the good his knowledge of the First Lady's pregnancy could do him professionally, he might as well be an insurance adjuster or the proprietor of a hardware store.

The fat man on his right woke up for a moment, or was talking in his sleep—it was hard to tell. "You know the thing about the President?" the fat man said, in a slurred voice. Becker was astonished. It was as if the fat man had been listening to his thoughts. "The thing about the President is that he's a pissant," the fat man said. "So are they all—all pissants." Then he went back to sleep, snoring bourbon-scented snores across the row of seats.

5 "This, Frederic, you will not believe."

Becker was still at the window, but his thoughts about the First Lady's pregnancy had gradually evaporated during close observation of an extraordinarily adroit messenger in the intersection below. While carrying four bulky packages and pressing a twenty-pound portable radio against his ear and making an obscene gesture to the purse peddler, the messenger had still managed to get a hand free to pinch a rather plain young woman who was about to cross the street. From the entrance line, Becker knew, without having to turn from the window, that Andy Wolferman, who wrote the Sports section, had just walked in carrying a piece of morning gossip. Wolferman was by far the most creative gossip at the magazine. Although he was always fully briefed on the sort of table-of-organization news that writers liked to discuss—speculation about who was likely to be banished to the chill splendor of Ottawa, where there was an opening for a bureau chief, or theories about who might have kept the Los Angeles bureau chief from being fired after it was revealed that the report he filed for the cover story on camping had been copied almost verbatim from a 1946 issue of *Boy's Life,* or predictions of who would replace Pete Smithers if the medical department ever diagnosed him as "too dumb to continue"—Wolferman usually dismissed such talk as "water fountain stuff." Andy Wolferman was a specialist in romance.

Once Wolferman and Becker and Pam Robinson, the Medicine section researcher, had devoted a lunch—a lunch that lasted until four-thirty—to estimating, in a systematic and carefully researched way, just how many romantic liaisons were going on among the editorial employees of the magazine at any given moment. According to a theory all three of them called Wolferman's Law, the number remained constant—some couples breaking up, some getting together, but the total always under the control of some deep, invariable anthropological law governing the percentage of matings among a certain number of culturally similar people brought into close contact over a certain number of hours every week. "Fellow scientists," Wolferman had said, as they got down to business, "the task we have set for ourselves is formidable." Fred Becker and Pam Robinson had nodded thoughtfully as Wolferman went through the difficulties facing them—the most serious of which was the remarkable discretion people at the magazine customarily employed in carrying on their romances. Even if the two people involved were both single—both people who would have described themselves as unfettered, enlightened, liberated adults who had the right to entangle themselves with anyone whose manner of tangling they enjoyed—they tended to handle their affair as if discovery would mean losing a child-custody fight or provoking a no-

toriously violent husband. It was not uncommon for an editor to react to the announcement of a marriage within the
staff by saying that he hadn't realized the two people involved knew each other. It was likely that the two had never
been seen together in bars or restaurants frequented by the
staff. In the office, they may have carried on whatever business they had together with a detachment bordering on
coldness. There was, though, a serious limitation to discretion: no matter how secretive the lovers tried to be, no matter how inventive they were in finding out-of-the-way bars
for tête-à-têtes and remote parks for walking hand in hand,
they always seemed to run into Andy Wolferman. More
than once, in answer to suspicions voiced by Fred Becker,
Wolferman had sworn that he never actually trailed people
from the office. He simply seemed to come across them.
The next morning, he would appear in Becker's office with a
report—a report that always began, "This, Frederic, you
will not believe."

At the historic lunch, Wolferman's phenomenal
string of chance encounters was not the only tool available
to the investigators. They had the freedom that came with
all of them having agreed even before the menus arrived to
betray everyone who had ever told them anything in strict-
est confidence. They had a pocket calculator with a ten-
digit read-out and memory functions. Becker and Pam
Robinson also had the advantage of being able to extrapo-
late from experience—having just ended, in the friendliest
sort of way, a short romance during which they would
occasionally meet for lunch at a truck stop on Eleventh
Avenue. Pam had been thrilled at the invitation to join
their commission of inquiry. She was a compact, blond,

enthusiastic, relentlessly cheerful young woman with the sort of air that would have been called "pert" in one generation and "game" in another. She tended to call people by some portion of their last name—so that Andy Wolferman became "Wolfs" or even "Wolfs-Babes."

Becker, who had assumed that receiving daily reports from Wolferman made him one of the best-informed writers at the magazine on such matters, was amazed that Pam knew of couples he had never suspected. "Did you get down Paula McGuire and Avery Duncan?" she said, after Wolferman took out a large, lined pad and began listing the names of couples they all knew about.

"Avery Duncan!" Becker said. "The copy boy?" Duncan was a slim young man who spoke in what Wolferman referred to as "a graduate student in comparative literature accent." He often dropped a quote from Rimbaud with the afternoon paper, and when he picked up copy he seemed to hold it at arm's length, as if it had a slight odor. "I thought he was gay."

"Wrong again," Pam said.

Becker shook his head in amazement—the first of many such headshakes he was to make that afternoon as Pam revealed to them what an assistant copy editor had revealed to her about two Business writers or Andy mentioned having run across the Science writer and a rather severe-looking proofreader at a dog track on Long Island. The waitresses, who had at first seemed irritated at having people linger over lunch past three or three-thirty, became curious about the proceedings and eventually gathered around the table, greeting each revelation with comments like "it just goes to show you" and "wouldn't you know it."

"Well, I guess that's it," Wolferman had finally said, totaling up the list.

"Nothing on the Bombshell?" Becker said. The Bombshell was a staggeringly voluptuous copy editor who had figured in the sexual fantasies of the magazine's writers for so long that the remarks they exchanged after she passed were normally limited to the latest setting in which they had imagined ravishing her. ("In Yankee Stadium," Wolferman would say, as they watched the Bombshell walk down the hall. "On a Sunday. Between games of a double-header. Thousands cheering.")

"Nothing that meets the standards of our inquiry," Wolferman said.

"You're sure you don't know anything about Syracuse Smiley?" Becker said.

"No eyewitness reports, I'm afraid," Wolferman said, writing down a figure and underlining it twice. "Here we have it. Not counting anything gay, we've got between sixteen and nineteen couples. According to my theory, that should be an eternal statistic."

"That sounds about right to me," Pam said. "You've got to say this, guys: there's a lot of action around here."

"I'm astonished," Becker said.

"What can be learned from a rigorous application of the scientific method never ceases to fill me with awe and wonder," Wolferman said. "We didn't even need the calculator."

"Too bad you've never come across Smiley somewhere," Becker said. "As much as you get around, you don't get around enough."

They had returned to the office pledged to gather for a

similar research session every six months—just to see if the number really did remain eternal, in accordance with Wolferman's Law—but the pledge had not been honored. Wolferman, though, had never given up his daily reports.

"I warn you—you're not going to believe this, Fred," he said again from the doorway.

"I think I'm going to believe it," Becker said, returning to the desk, "as bizarre and mind-boggling as it's going to sound."

"I thought I might find you at Medicine instead of over here, by the way," Wolferman said. "Doc Kennedy is looking marginally terminal."

"Yeah, Pam told me he's been struck by the dread snail poo-poo."

"I just saw him in the elevator, and he seemed to be heading for medical," Wolferman said. "He had a thermometer sticking out of his mouth—that was my clue. Might have had one sticking out of his tushie too, for all I know. It was hard to tell because he had his pants on for a change. It did look kind of lumpy back there though."

"As a matter of fact, he usually is sprouting two thermometers," Becker said. "He told me once that was the only way to make sure of getting an absolutely accurate reading. He goes down to medical every Monday morning, though. Pam was talking as if he might recover."

"He's a terrifying example to us all," Wolferman said. "I'm afraid I'll be sitting in my office writing about some lunatic jogger one of these weeks and suddenly find myself winded and stinking with sweat and with dog shit all over my shoes." Although he had written the Sports section for several years, Wolferman, whose thin shoulders and thick glasses gave him a scholarly look, was not an exercise enthu-siast. In fact, the most positive statement he had ever made about athletics in private conversation was, "I suppose it's a nice thing for the goyim."

For a moment, Becker thought of asking Wolderman's advice about what to do with the information he had been given about the First Lady. Wolferman had a good grasp of tactics, and, in evaluating the information, he would have the advantage of knowing Leonard Wentzell. The three of them had spent a couple of boozy evenings in New York once when Wentzell had been in town "on a little project." Becker had prepared for the evening by giving Wolferman the usual disclaimer on the Rug Merchant ("He's a little, well, unusual, but, you know, if you go all through grade school with someone. . . ."), but it had turned out to be unnecessary. Wolferman thought Wentzell was remarkably entertaining—he particularly liked the Merchant's "pidgin Yiddish"—and Wentzell had paid Wolferman the ultimate compliment of letting on that he suspected him of being an operative of the French Deuxième Bureau.

"Anyway, here is what you are not going to believe," Wolferman said, breaking into Becker's thoughts. "There I was last night at Joe Horn Dimey's Bar, in Washington Heights—"

"Wait a minute, Andy," Becker said. "May I ask what you were doing in Washington Heights?" Becker was not even certain where Washington Heights was, but he knew it was a long way from Murray Hill, where Andy Wolferman lived.

"I had just dropped into Joe Horn Dimey's Bar," Wolferman said, "to cash a check."

"Why would a bar in Washington Heights cash your check?"

"Honest face and a respectable suit of clothing," Wolferman said.

"It makes perfect sense. I'm sorry I asked." It certainly made as much sense as Wolferman's having been in the lingerie department of Bloomingdales–White Plains one Saturday at the same time Peg Freedson, a Business section researcher who had once been a nationally ranked tennis player, was picking out slinky nightgowns in the company of a wan Doc Kennedy. It made as much sense as Wolferman's having been at a Portuguese restaurant near the Newark Airport when Rob Rowan, the Religion writer—who, as far as anyone at the magazine knew, spent his off-hours discussing the Curia with dissident priests from Latin America—walked in hand in hand with Pete Smithers' secretary, Genine McIntyre, a lavishly dressed and carefully made-up young woman known around the office as La Contessa.

"Anyway, there I was, conducting my simple financial transaction, when who—or perhaps whom—did I happen to—"

The telephone rang, and Becker picked it up. It was Genine McIntyre informing him that he was late for story conference.

"Christ. I lost track of time," he said, as he gathered up the suggestions and his clipboard. "We'll have to continue at lunch, Andy."

"I will be happy to continue my tale at lunch, Fred," Wolferman said. "But I warn you: you will not believe it."

6 Pete Smithers was leaning back in his chair, at the angle he had made his own. His heels were somehow hooked on the edge of the desk. For the half-dozen people seated in his office, waiting for the Lifestyle story conference to begin, the bottoms of Pete Smithers' shoes were the only part of him visible, although a clipboard he was holding on his lap occasionally bobbed into view. Becker noticed that Smithers' Bass Weejuns were either new or resoled. Smithers' voice seemed to emerge from somewhere below the desk: "All right, Fred, whatta we got for the folks this week?"

Becker looked over his clipboard—a signal for the others at the meeting to adjust their own clipboards, ready to list the stories Smithers accepted. Sitting with Becker in Smithers' office were Carol Goodenow, the Lifestyle researcher; Keith Johnson, a quiet man from the wire desk; two photo researchers (for reasons unknown to Becker, photo researchers, like FBI men and nuns, traveled in pairs); and Genine McIntyre, Smithers' secretary.

"Well, we've got the one from California about people drowning in hot-tubs," Becker said.

"Is that a trend?" the voice from behind Smithers' desk said.

"I don't know if you can call it a trend, exactly, Pete," Becker said. "It's not really at the point of being the thing to do in California, or anything like that. More of a phenomenon than a trend. I guess people just get all relaxed in there, and smoke a little something, and chant their mantras, and get in touch with their bodies, or maybe lose touch with their bodies—and they sort of slip beneath the waves."

"Didn't we already do drowning in hot-tubs?" Smithers said. "Genine?"

"Scalding in hot-tubs," Genine said. "We did a sixtyliner on scalding in hot-tubs last year. Some of the people who were scalded did drown, but it was a scalding piece really, not a drowning piece."

"I thought I remembered a piece we did on drowning in hot-tubs," Smithers said.

Becker shrugged. It did seem as if everything to be written about hot-tubs had already appeared in the Lifestyle section. He himself had done one story on new hot-tub designs and another story on a study showing that the subject most discussed by people sitting in hot-tubs in Marin County, California, without any clothes on was real estate.

"Drowning in waterbeds," Genine said. "Scalding in hot-tubs."

"Put it on the list," Smithers said.

Everyone in the room listed the hot-tubs piece on his or her clipboard. The two photo researchers compared clipboards to make certain they had the same wording. "What else we got, Fred?" Smithers said.

"Well, there's this two-thirds stocking story, also from California."

"Tell me more about that one," Smithers said. "Does that mean they're wearing two-thirds of a stocking? Which two thirds? What's the point, anyway?"

"Well, I don't know too much about it," Becker said. He was actually hoping that Smithers would decide to drop the two-thirds stocking story. He didn't much like doing fashion stories. What he really wanted to say was that it might make sense to wait until Trish Webster, who was sometimes detached from the Entertainment Arts section to do fashion pieces for Lifestyle, happened to be available. He knew, though, that suggesting a woman writer for a women's fashions story would upset Carol Goodenow, who was the chairperson of the magazine's Women Employees Committee. When Carol was upset, she often started to cry. That upset her even more, given her belief that women are no more likely to burst into tears than men are, so once she started crying there was almost no stopping her. Becker liked Carol Goodenow, and he tried to avoid doing anything that might upset her. "As I understand it," he went on, "it's not really about wearing two-thirds of a stocking. I don't think. It's more like two-thirds length. Two-thirds of the way up the leg. Or maybe two-thirds of the way to the knee."

"Two-thirds stockings! Jesus!" came Smithers' voice from behind and below the desk.

"I guess it really doesn't sound all that interesting," Becker said. He glanced over at Carol Goodenow. He thought he had seen her lower lip start to quiver, but he might have been imagining it. "I mean, I guess we're about due for a stocking story," he went on, trying to make certain Carol didn't think that he was sounding negative just because the story had to do with women's fashions. "I'm just not sure this is it."

"Let's scratch it," Smithers said.

Marks were made on clipboards. Nobody said anything for a moment or two. Smithers' desk chair creaked. The Countess adjusted one of her eyelashes. Keith Johnson, the wire-desk man, looked as if he might fall asleep.

"Then there's this thirty-liner on obscene topiary that was written last week but didn't run," Becker said.

There was another short period of silence. Finally, the voice from behind the desk said, "Obscene topiary?" Smithers, who had scheduled and edited the story the previous week, had apparently forgotten what it was about.

"Dirty bushes," Becker said, working on the theory that the simplest explanation was always best for Smithers.

"In the bushes?"

"No, dirty bushes—bushes made into statues with, well, sexual overtones." Becker looked over to see if his careful choice of words had succeeded in refreshing Smithers' memory without embarrassing Carol Goodenow, who was made uncomfortable by talk of sex in public. Carol was blushing slightly.

"Didn't we do dirty bushes?" Smithers said. "Genine?"

"Last week we did dirty bushes, but it didn't run," Genine said. "A thirty-liner. Spaced out by that piece on grownups chewing bubble gum."

"Put it on the list," Smithers' voice said.

"Then Cravens, in Indianapolis, suggests a story on this little town in central Indiana that's supposed to be the sex change capital of the world," Becker said.

"Jesus!" Smithers said. "Dirty bushes. Sex changes. This is getting to be the goddamned Porno section. Isn't that a Medicine story?"

"Well, Cravens slugged it Lifestyle or Medicine. He thinks the real story is that this little town that used to be a limestone quarrying town was down on its luck because not many buildings made out of limestone are being built these days. And then this doctor there started doing a lot of sex change operations and it became a sort of cottage industry—renting out rooms for people to live in while they're waiting for their breasts to grow, that sort of thing. Kind of put the town on the map again. Now, apparently, other things are happening with their economic development committee, although I notice Cravens doesn't say exactly what."

"Jesus!" Smithers said again.

"I hear Medicine's going to be all taken up this week with this big wrap-up on the pancreas they're doing," Becker said, beginning to wonder, despite himself, precisely where the pancreas was. "So maybe we can grab this one."

Smithers mumbled something that sounded as if it might have been "goddamned queers," but it was hard to be certain. Carol Goodenow, her embarrassment over the subject temporarily put aside, leaned forward, apparently at the ready to take down any addition Smithers might provide to a list she kept of remarks he had made that were offensive to one group or another. It was a long list. Many of the remarks on it sounded rather dated. When stories about homosexuals came up in Lifestyle story conferences, Smithers was likely to become visibly red in the face—

visibly, that is, if someone happened to be standing up directly in front of his desk and was thus able to peer down at him through the other end of the gunsight—and mutter something like "pansies" or "goddamned fairies." At a story conference for Entertainment Arts, another section Smithers presided over, a proposed story about a gay production of *Romeo and Juliet*—with Romeo as a bartender in a leather bar and Jules as a swish interior decorator—had brought Smithers forward in his desk chair with a crack so sharp that most of those at the conference dropped their clipboards. "The queers are everywhere!" he had shouted, as he arrived abruptly at a more conventional posture—sitting upright behind his desk, as Bob Bingham, the Entertainment Arts writer, later put it, "like a normal human being."

"Apparently he isn't very good at it—the doctor," Becker went on. "From what Cravens says, it sounds like people are always drifting into Indianapolis for repairs. I don't know exactly what the problems are. Cravens says something about 'things not on as well as they might be.' " As he outlined the story to Smithers, Becker began to think that it might be only marginally preferable to a long wrap-up on the pancreas. "We could get into legal problems, I guess, mentioning that sort of thing," he added.

Keith Johnson, who had never spoken a word in a story conference, as far as Becker could remember, suddenly blurted out, "I guess that's why they wear their pants tucked inside their boots out that way," and started to cackle. Great grunts of laughter came from behind Smithers' desk. The photo researchers began giggling. Carol Goodenow had turned scarlet. Becker was afraid she might simply bolt from the office, but she seemed to be keeping her seat by an effort of will.

"Pants tucked in!" Smithers yelped from behind the desk. "Put it on the list. Christ knows whether Woody'll let it in the magazine, but at least I'll be able to spend the week reading what Cravens files. Is that all?"

"Well, there's this suggestion about disco banks," Becker said.

"That's a Business story," Smithers said abruptly.

"We did disco banks last March," La Contessa said.

"It's still a Business story," Smithers said. "Jesus! disco banks! The queers are everywhere."

7 "Well, Jack," Woody Fenton said. "What do we have for the folks this week?"

Fenton was leaning back in his office chair at a moderate angle, with his legs crossed. His clipboard was resting lightly on his desk. The magazine having assigned desks in sizes corresponding to rank, the managing editor had one about the size of a ping-pong table. Late one closing night, after Woody Fenton had finally gone home to Mamaroneck, a dippy copy boy and two drunken copy editors had held a roller derby on the managing editor's desk. Andy Wolferman always claimed that when he had his first audience with Fenton, upon joining the magazine, the managing editor started to come out from behind his desk, presumably to shake hands, but forgot the purpose of the journey by the time he finished it—with the result that he simply stood in front of Wolferman, looked him up and down, and said "Golly."

Fastened to the desk was the terminal for an intercom system that had been installed during the regime of the previous managing editor, Walter Heinlich—an abrupt, humorless man known among the writers and researchers as the Hun. The intercom system connected the managing editor's office with the offices of the eight senior editors—who, at the time, were often said to have been chosen according to how frightened they were of Heinlich. The intercom system itself had its frightening aspect: when the managing editor flipped the button connecting him to, say, Pete Smithers' office, the signal summoning Smithers to the small black box on his own, somewhat more modest, desk was a horrifying drone that had been compared to the sound of two hundred industrial vacuum cleaners in chorus. Senior editors tended to be vigilant about not keeping the managing editor waiting—even after the Hun was succeeded by the amiable Woody Fenton. During Heinlich's reign, the senior editor in charge of the Business section leaped so quickly toward the intercom from a couch, where he had been studying some cables, that he fell over a low coffee table and broke his ankle. The managing editor's console signaled the presence of a senior editor on the line with the sort of soft chime that is sometimes heard as a summons to floorwalkers in a particularly posh department store.

"Well, we've got the secretary of state on the cover again, Woody," Jack Thompson said. At the beginning of each week, just after the story conferences in the sections were over, Thompson and Ralph Holbrook and Max Eisen, the chief of correspondents, met with Fenton in his office. Thompson always read the list of what had been scheduled for the week—all of it scheduled, of course, subject to the approval of the managing editor. No one had ever been able to figure out what else Jack Thompson did; the writers sometimes referred to him as Assistant Managing Editor for Reading the List.

"We've already got forty pages of Rappaport's file in from Washington," Max Eisen said. "We've got files coming from ten overseas bureaus. With the general strike in England, we'll probably charter a jet to get Maddox's file to the telex in Paris." Eisen, a dapper man who was known for the ease with which he spent the magazine's money, loved to charter airplanes. On scheduled flights, he always went first class—he expected his correspondents to do the same— but he tended to refer to even first-class travel on a regular airline rather disparagingly as "going commercial."

"I like the secretary of state," Fenton said. "Good guy."

Holbrook and Eisen both nodded.

"He gives a hell of a briefing," Fenton went on. "Really swell. Remember that briefing he gave during the last Southeast Asia business, Ralph?"

"I wasn't at that briefing, Woody," Holbrook said. "You and Max went down for that one, and I was minding the store."

"Right. That's right," Fenton said. "I love that board room they have at State. Great paneling. One thing you've got to say for the guys at State, they know paneling."

Holbrook nodded. "They're good at it," he said.

"You know who gave great briefings?" Fenton said.

The other three shook their heads.

"Westmoreland," Fenton said. "Westy. I loved those briefings. In Saigon. He'd get you up on the roof of one of those buildings and show you the rows of tanks and choppers. Golly, I love choppers."

"Hell of a machine," Holbrook said.

"We had a chopper in the Saigon bureau," said Eisen,

who enjoyed buying various sorts of conveyances as much as he enjoyed chartering them.

"I remember that chopper," Fenton said.

"Two choppers, really," Eisen said. "A chopper and a back-up chopper. I hated to see them go. When Saigon fell, all I could think about was that those little bastards got both my choppers."

"Good food, too," Fenton said. "Westmoreland put on super briefings in every way. Lots of maps. Overlays on maps. Gosh!"

The others nodded, uncertain whether the "gosh" applied to the irony of a commander whose briefings were that good being defeated in the field or to the wonders of map overlays.

"Shame about that White House briefing, Ralph," Fenton said.

"Well, those things happen, Woody," Holbrook replied, withdrawing his pipe from the side pocket of his jacket.

"Funny, that was the first time we've been asked," Fenton said. "I know we've given the President a hard time on the wildlife thing, but still—. Anything scheduled on the President's wife being ill?"

Thompson looked up and down the list. "No, nothing in National News," he said. "And I didn't see anything on the wires. Medicine's got nothing but the pancreas."

"Guess it wasn't serious," Fenton said. He reached over to a rack on his vast desk, picked up a pipe, and, to Holbrook's astonishment, started puffing on it successfully without relighting it. "Do you know how many times Heinlich was briefed at the White House?" he asked.

"I don't think so, Woody," Holbrook said.

"Fourteen times," Fenton said. "Fourteen times. That's something."

"It sure is," Holbrook said.

"That's a lot of times," Eisen said.

Fenton puffed on his pipe for a while, and then said, "Wow!"

8 Fred Becker had come to New York to sing in musical comedy. He was twenty-three, although, to his constant irritation, he didn't quite look it. "You look too much like Ensign Pulver and not enough like Mr. Roberts," Wentzell had told him at the time, attempting to persuade him to abandon his theatrical ambitions and accept a job with an import-export firm that seemed sufficiently bogus to be a front for at least one intelligence service and possibly a money-washing operation. Becker, though, could not be swayed. He had no interest in import-export or in money washing. For that matter, he had no interest in being an actor in straight plays or the sort of singer who entertains in nightclubs and concerts. He wanted to sing nowhere but on the musical comedy stage. While he was going through the usual voice lessons and acting lessons and auditions and showcases, he supported himself by working as a newsmagazine copy boy. The job required no thinking. The hours often allowed him freedom for lessons and auditions during the day. The money was as good as it would have been if he had worked as a waiter or in one of the other traditional jobs for aspiring actors in New York. Ev-

erything had worked out rather well except the musical comedy. Becker had plugged away for a couple of years, but then, at the auditions for a road company tour of *Music Man,* he was taken aside by the casting director, a gruff but fatherly man named Syd Berg.

"You have a nice voice, sonny," Berg said, after calling Becker off the stage and offering him a seat in the nearly deserted theater.

"Thanks very much," Becker said, although the tone of Berg's voice had made the compliment sound not quite complimentary.

"Did you happen to notice the cleaning lady dusting the seats in about the fourteenth row while you were singing?"

Becker nodded.

"You may have thought she wasn't paying any attention to you because she was concentrating on her dusting," Berg went on. "Or because she hears so much singing it's become like Muzak to her. Or because she is not a connoisseur of the musical stage. Wrong. I've seen her put down her dusting rag and applaud if she's really impressed. I've seen her hold her nose when she thinks somebody up there stinks."

For just a moment—for the last moment in his musical comedy career—Becker clutched at a straw: the cleaning lady had not, after all, held her nose, and Berg had definitely used the phrase "nice voice."

"I'll tell you why she wasn't paying any attention to you, sonny," Berg said. "She couldn't hear you. She was dusting the fourteenth row, and you carry to about the twelfth. You have a nice voice, sonny, but the last of the belt-'em-out singers you are not. Do yourself a favor—do me a favor, because I like to do one mitzvah a year; this is a nasty business—go into another line of work."

Becker knew that Syd Berg was telling the truth—knew it in a way that made him realize he had, without facing up to it, known the truth himself for some time. His musical comedy career came to an end that afternoon. He didn't go back to Nebraska, though. He had, just a week before, found a rent-controlled apartment, and he simply couldn't bear to leave it. Looking for it had, at one point, become virtually a full-time job—rising early to search for the ambulances and police cars that might indicate an opening caused by a fatal heart attack, cultivating sullen West Side elevator men during the lank hours of the afternoon, showing up at Times Square late at night to get a jump on the ads in the early edition of the morning paper—and he was not about to abandon it just as the payoff arrived. The apartment seemed reason enough to remain in the city: for a few months after his watershed confrontation with Syd Berg, he tended to answer the standard cocktail party inquiry "What do you do?" by saying, "I live in a rent-controlled apartment."

He was still working as a copy boy a couple of months later when Walter Heinlich, in what Andy Wolferman had called "one of his periodic spasms of democracy," decided that the opportunity to try out as writers should be extended to some people like copy boys and proofreaders. As it turned out, Fred Becker was very good at newsmagazine writing. He had a knack for structure and compression, and he could write uncluttered declarative sentences that carried the story from paragraph to paragraph. Before long, he was writing the Benchmarks section, a listing of the week's marriages and divorces and deaths—a task that made him realize he could have saved himself a lot of frigid searches for ambulances during his apartment-hunting days if he had only thought to cultivate newspaper obituary writers instead of West Side elevator operators. Then he put in a couple of months writing Editor's Note, a column next to the table of contents which the writers called Eisen's Follies, since it consisted almost entirely of stories about the exploits of the magazine's correspondents in gathering the week's news. ("As Mexico City bureau chief Diego Pearce was briefed by the Mexican foreign minister over a breakfast of *huevos rancheros* and orange juice, Jake Bernstein of the Dallas bureau was arranging to rent the top four floors of the office building that offered the best view of what was going on in the closely guarded compound of the Canadian embassy.")

Eventually, he became a floater in the back of the book, and there, he had made it clear, was where he wanted to stay. The management of the magazine considered a regular writing slot to be a higher calling than floating, but Becker dreaded the thought of eternal Science or eternal Sports or, most numbing of all, eternal Cyprus. He was not much interested in upward movement on the masthead, but he liked the horizontal movement that could mean writing about the Gross National Product as an economic indicator one week for the Business section and as a neo–punk-rock group the next week for the Music section.

He had been tempted to leave only when the movement seemed in danger of stopping. His tour as a reporter in Washington was supposed to have lasted a year—"an important arrow to have in your quiver," Ralph Holbrook had informed him, with a smile. Although the magazine's top editors did not seem to be deeply committed to the reports they received every week from their bureaus—a casual remark by the defense secretary in the magazine's executive dining room could undercut months of research by a reporter—they often spoke of the importance of having been a reporter. They looked on reporting the way army generals looked on leading combat troops as a line officer: it was a good thing to have done until one became too important to do it. After a couple of months in Washington being lied to by a variety of middle-level bureaucrats—a period he loathed not merely because he knew he was being lied to but also because, as it happened, he did not like telephoning strangers under any circumstances—he was about to quit the magazine, return to New York, reclaim his old apartment (which he had, in violation of the rent control laws, sublet), and enjoy the simple pleasures of living in it as an occupation until something else came along. He was saved from that drastic step by the magazine's desperate need for someone to stand in for Rob Rowan, the regular Religion writer—a Catholic intellectual who was away from the office for weeks because of what Leonard Wentzell had diagnosed from afar as Communion Wafer Spotted Fever. Becker had floated ever since.

Because it was considered important for the section's writer to work somewhere near its researcher and its senior editor, a floater usually moved physically to the office of whichever writer he was replacing—in the manner, Bryan Murray, the other floater, always said, of a visiting nurse. When Murray moved, he needed the help of one of the grocery carts the copyboys used to deliver newspapers and interoffice mail. He carried along with him half a dozen pictures of a family so large that Murray himself didn't seem to know how many children he had. ("Many; oh, many," he would usually say when asked.) He also had as part of his kit a dart board, a pile of magazines, several huge envelopes that held old stories and unanswered letters, a bust of Mao Tse-tung, and a couple of hundred manuscript pages of an autobiography he was ghosting in his spare time for a merchant banker who was known outside his field mainly for having amassed the world's largest collection of prom programs. The research material and tape recordings from which Murray was supposedly writing the book, *This Dance Is Mine,* were kept in his basement in Montclair; he always said that having them available for reference while he wrote the book during spare moments at the office would be "sissy stuff."

Fred Becker carried with him only a small, expandable cardboard file that never had much in it beyond a small collection of Woody Fenton's golly memos—which Becker kept on the theory that they were either historic or too bizarre to dispose of. The offices he moved in and out of did not vary in basic design. Each writer had a ten-by-ten square with a gray metal desk and a formica-covered typing table and one nonopening window and off-white cork walls whose receptivity to pushpins encouraged writers to tack up anything that struck their fancy—with the result that the average office looked like what Bryan Murray had described as "the cell of a hip monk." A memo from Ralph Holbrook asking that writers show some restraint in the sort of pictures and posters and souvenirs they pinned on the wall—a memo written just after a cleaning woman entering the office of Henry Nagle, the Science writer, late one night had been seriously frightened by a decoration that Nagle described as "perfectly normal in parts of the Amazon"—had been pinned up as part of the decor by some writers, but otherwise ignored.

Because of the variety of decor, Becker found that what he did while thinking of the next sentence varied according to what section he was writing. When he wrote Education, he constantly crumpled up copy paper and tried his luck at a miniature basketball hoop that Milt Silvers, the Education writer, had mounted on the wastepaper basket. Surrounded by souvenirs of papal tours while he put in what seemed to be an interminable period of service in Religion, he began experimenting with a new sort of hagiography, assigning saints lives that reflected the modern connotations of their names—so that San Tropez became a young beach-boy who perished by using his own body to protect two sleeping starlets and a bisexual advertising executive from the scorching Mediterranean sun, and St. Thomas was a duty-free liquor-store clerk who met a grisly end when he tried to close the shop at five o'clock, as he had been instructed to do, even though some of the tourists present had not yet bought their full exemption. The office of the regular Lifestyle writer, Roger Burnside, had a view of one of the busiest intersections in midtown, and Becker found that he often spent his time in Lifestyle staring out the window, trying to imagine what was being said by the newsdealer who was shaking his head at someone who seemed to be asking for change for a quarter ("This look like the Chase Manhattan Bank, lady?") or by the young woman who was speaking intently to the young man walking alongside her

("Tommy, what you're suggesting is the most disgusting thing I've ever heard.").

Roger Burnside's decor was dominated by his memo collection, which was particularly strong in silly and often ungrammatical memos from management. The only trophy on Burnside's wall that Becker reread every time he wrote the Lifestyle section was a Xerox of Charlie Sayler's most astoundingly prescient prediction memo. Charlie Sayler was a National News Writer of dour temperament who was known for the calm with which he assumed the worst. He maintained what Andy Wolferman always called "an oriental fatalism" about what happened to his copy. Whenever Sayler was assigned to write a cover story, he began by composing what he called a prediction memo, which predicted in detail what would happen day-by-day as the story got written and rewritten and edited and, finally, put to press. Then he would have the prediction memo dated and notarized by the newsdealer in the lobby, place it in a sealed envelope, and leave it in the care of Marge Hector, the head researcher of the National News section—a former Wac who had terrified writer and editor alike for twenty years. When the writers and researchers of National News gathered on Friday night to celebrate the section's closing, Marge Hector would ceremoniously remove the prediction memo from its envelope and read it to the assembled crowd—accompanied by gasps and cheers as the actual events of the week popped up with amazing regularity.

Restless after the Lifestyle story conference, Becker walked over to the wall to read the prediction memo Burnside had saved—a memo written just before Sayler began a cover story on the secretary of state:

"Monday. I arrive at office to find that Loyal Researcher has already put on desk fourteen books on diplomacy, with relevant pages noted by paper clips, plus eight inches of newspaper clippings. I put all of these on floor in the corner so there's room to work on desk. Ace Washington reporter Marvin Rappaport has already started filing main report on Sec. of State. His first take of 30 pages is already on desk. I plan to read that, then get to pile in corner, but first I must read & digest 4,000-word memo from Beloved Senior Editor, Martin Baron, on what should be in 4,000-word cover story. Baron is worried that if cover story turns out to be weak Sec. of State will be pushed off cover by Archbishop of Canterbury, who's being heavily promoted by Ed Winstead, wily & beloved senior editor in charge of Religion. There is a rumor that Baron, who hates non–National News cover stories, has whispered to Holbrook to whisper to Woody that British P. M. considers Archbishop of Canterbury a lightweight. I get time to read 1st take from Rappaport late in the afternoon. The pile in corner remains untouched.

"Tuesday. I arrive to find 2nd Rappaport take of 35 pages on desk. I get halfway through when 3rd take of 40 pages arrives. Does Rappaport never sleep? I ask myself. Also have 20 pages from Chicago bureau on Sec. of State's boyhood & college. 30 pages from Paris on what French Pres. thinks of Sec.'s taste in wine, etc. 50 total from other capitals. 30 fm San Francisco on ex-wife's playing around with kinky crowd. I read that one. Very good stuff. Loyal Researcher comes in with six more inches of clippings. I thank LR profusely, and make new pile in another corner of my office.

"Wednesday. I arrive at office, Toss hat on 1st pile in corner. Start writing. 50 more pages arrive from Rappaport. Man has no mercy, no shame, no sense of perspective. I put new 50 on 2nd pile. I still feel confident I've read a lot more of Rappaport's file than Baron, who has files for other stories in section to read, also is notoriously slow reader. Baron interrupts my writing often to say he's worried. Winstead has apparently told Woody that Archbishop should be on the cover that week, since he has tricky ticker nobody knows about and could drop dead anytime. Baron is very pissed off at Winstead's dirty pool. Says Archbishop is healthy as a mule, also that smart. I write my heart out. I eat at my desk (multi-ethnic special from Manny's Deli: chopped-liver & bacon on pita). Heartburn awful. 10 P.M. I finish.

"Thursday. Baron says story is great. Also, he wants me to write it over again. I figure he wants to make sure if Woody doesn't like it Baron will be able to say at least it's a big improvement over first version. Shows he's on the job. I do new version, with more numbers in lead (Baron likes numbers in lead; once worked for Wall St. Journal). Also, I jiggle paragraphs around a lot. 30 more pages arrive from Rappaport. I put them on 1st pile in the corner, on top of my hat. Baron says the new version is great. Then he rewrites it, including two paragraphs saying Sec. of State not strong enough supporter of international wildlife preservation—anticipating Woody's interest in favorite cause of Big Boss Towndsend. Baron's writing is very fluid, since he is not saddled by complicated facts burdening anyone who has read large hunks of Rappaport's file. Baron initials story, sends it on to Woody. I am so grateful I tip him off to

San Francisco file on playing around with kinky crowd. 40 more pages arrive from Rappaport.

"Woody says he loves the story. Then he says to write it over again. Wants less on Sec. of State being soft on destroyers of wildlife. (I figure he wants to please BB Towndsend but not piss off Sec. of State so much that Sec. of State will quit inviting him to private briefings.) I take out 2 of Baron's wildlife paragraphs. Baron puts 1 back in, takes out one of mine. I jiggle paragraphs. He jiggles them back. Sends it to Woody, Woody wants new version. Says it needs spark. I put in spark, also couple of paragraphs I had taken out before. Baron to Woody. Woody writes in 2 paragraphs on world peace he heard at a dinner party from British ambassador when British ambassador was shitfaced drunk & even more pompous than usual. Then he writes in a paragraph about the Third World that somebody stuck in his ear at the Nairobi Airport when he took tour of African and Middle East bureaus. Then he says he loves the story. Congratulates me. Tells me I'm a wiz.

"Friday. LR starts checking the story, true to her Researcher's Oath to produce a source supporting every fact in story and to find some reason why any sentence suspected of being even remotely graceful must be changed in a way that makes it boring or awkward. Checking takes 7 hours and 24 minutes. LR cries twice. I cry once. Sec. of State would cry if he could see what was happening. Names LR calls me: egomaniac (twice), fool, sloppiest writer in section, a person with no regard whatsoever for the truth, dumb shithead. Names I call LR: Queen of the Nitpickers (14 times). LR, tired of arguing with me, tells Most Beloved Head Researcher, Marge Hector, stuff Woody wrote in is irrelevant and distorts meaning of the story if included. MBHR Marge Hector says, 'Relevant my ass! Does it check or doesn't it?' Finally, story, checked to its teeth, is put on the wire of the Washington bureau as a courtesy to Rappaport—so he'll have advance notice of what his sources are going to hate him for. I brush some papers off my hat & get ready to go out to dinner. Phone call from Rappaport. 'Great story,' he says. 'Did you get my file?' "

Becker walked over to Roger Burnside's desk and sat down. Who would be on the cover, he wondered, if the story Wentzell had told him was a cover story? The President? The First Lady? The baby? The obstetrician? It was still not clear, of course, that what Wentzell told him was even true. Becker had already taken the first step toward finding out. That morning he had phoned one of the few good friends he made during his imprisonment in the Washington bureau—Duane Williams, the Washington correspondent for a chain of newspapers in the wheat belt. Williams was a thoroughly competent reporter, but his journalistic curiosity could be piqued only by tips that seemed to hold the promise of agricultural scandal or a drastic change in farm price supports. Becker, without saying why he wanted to know, had asked Williams to find out if there seemed to be anything odd about the First Lady's schedule or behavior. Then what? Even if Becker did manage to confirm the First Lady's pregnancy—a process that would presumably require calling strangers on the telephone—what would he do with the information? Could he present it to Fenton on the condition that he never be promoted for having obtained it? If Fenton wasn't interested—he often seemed wary of stories that had not appeared in the newspapers first—could Becker take his business elsewhere? For a while, Becker had been nibbled at by a rival newsmagazine's headhunter, but he found the prospect of moving unappealing. The headhunter—a laconic, depressingly jaded assistant managing editor who lunched on vodka martinis—was unable to guarantee that Becker would not find his efforts rewarded with a permanent slot in World News, and he persisted in referring to "our shop" and "your shop" as if they were discussing auto-body repair operations.

Becker wondered why Wentzell might have leaked him a story that turned out not to be true. It was always possible, of course, that Wentzell was a CIA agent—a possibility Becker would be thoroughly convinced of, he knew, only when the Commies held the grain exchange—and the CIA, for some devious reason of its own, wanted to embarrass the President. Of course, Wentzell might be serving some purpose of his own by leaking information that was false. Wentzell was obviously capable of leaking false information for no particular purpose at all—at least none that could be divined by the general run of people outside the city limits of Shmata Grande, Jalisco. What Wentzell had told him might be pure fiction, unadulterated even by being part of some vaguely rational conspiracy.

Pure fiction, Becker thought, as he stood up and walked over to the window. What if Wentzell's tip was pure fiction? What if it was not part of some carefully orchestrated scheme but simply a notion that floated into Wentzell's mind as part of one of his wacky little "projects"? Did that mean it was useless? Or could it be written as fiction? Might it be the material for one of those block-buster Washington novels that had made so many people rich? Standing at the window, Becker realized that the title of a novel had come into his head: *The President's Wife Is Pregnant.*

A lot of the huge sums paid for Washington novels had, of course, gone to people who were already famous for their participation in the Watergate crimes. ("No wonder they couldn't run the country," Pete Smithers had said. "A bunch of sissy novelists.") But there had been a couple of huge paperback sales of Washington novels written by people who, as far as Becker knew, had no claim to criminality beyond some insignificant misdemeanors. Suddenly, Becker could see the opening scene. It is set in the Cabinet Room or the Map Room or wherever important meetings are held in White House novels. (He could find that out by asking Rappaport in the Washington bureau, or, better yet, by reading one of the Washington novels.) The members of the cabinet are there. Also the head of the National Security Council and the Army Chief of Staff. What is the Army Chief of Staff doing there? Certainly the solution arrived at—whatever it is—will not be military. Of course, the President's family always uses Walter Reed Hospital. Walter Reed Navy Hospital. Well, the Navy Chief of Staff is there—described down to the ribbons on his chest and a slight limp he picked up in the Battle of Leyte from kicking a Philippine messboy. The chair at the head of the table is empty. Everyone is awaiting the President, but the President does not arrive. Somebody else arrives instead. Maybe the Secretary of State—the old-fashioned, Ivy League, Wall Street, Council on Foreign Relations, High

Episcopalian Secretary of State. He stands quietly at the head of the table until the chatter among the cabinet secretaries grows still. The Secretary of State remains silent for some time—glancing around the room for effect, as he had been taught many years before by the debate coach at the St. Paul's School. Then he says, in the round, almost English tones that are his trademark, "Gentlemen, the President's wife is pregnant."

If the book made hundreds of thousands of dollars, Becker reflected, he might even be able to keep most of it. His former wife, Greta, once one of the few radical communards on the East Coast with an almost evangelical belief in the institution of alimony as the cornerstone of the American family, had adopted a course of such independence that he hadn't heard from her in four years. With all of the blockbuster's profits for himself, Becker could presumably quit his job as a back-of-the-book floater. That was the goal of writers all around him—to be tapped by what Wolferman called "the golden claw," and be able to say goodbye forever to arbitrary editors and late-night closings and Syracuse Smiley. On Monday and Tuesdays, before enough raw material had arrived for them to begin writing the week's stories, their typewriters clattered away at historical novels and screen treatments and T.V. sitcom pilots. Becker, though, was not certain that he wanted to leave the magazine. Once he had resigned himself to the fact that he was never going to play Curly in the big Broadway revival of *Oklahoma,* he had found floating a rather pleasant way to make a living. He had never quite got over feeling that he was rather lucky to be where he was: if he had worked as a waiter rather than as a copy boy during his acting days, after all, he might have ended up as a maître d'.

9 "You coming?" Andy Wolferman said. He was standing at the door of the office with Charlie Sayler, who was, as usual, looking melancholy. Bryan Murray, the other floater, joined them, pulling on his coat.

"I guess," Becker said, reaching for his coat. "Does Rocco have Milt on the phone?"

"Rocco's out sick," Wolferman said.

Becker hesitated. "Milt'll grab us on the way to the elevator, sure as hell," he said.

"We have a new route," Murray said. "In the back door of the copy room and through the photo lab. It's kind of a pain in the ass, but we can get to the elevator without passing his office at all."

"Why couldn't Rocco call him from home?" Becker asked, as he joined the others in the hall.

"Well, for one thing, Rocco's probably not out sick at home," Wolferman said. "He's probably out sick at the track."

"Well, I guess we can try it," Becker said. "We can't skip lunch every time Rocco wants to go to the track." Becker was not confident of making it to the elevator without encountering Milt Silvers, the Education writer. Ordinarily, Rocco Popolizio, one of the copy boys, working under a small retainer that provided him with some two-dollar-bets money, telephoned Silvers whenever Wolferman and Becker and their usual lunch crowd were about to head toward the elevator. Silvers tended to face the window rather than the door when he talked on the phone, allowing them to dash past his door one at a time—like commandos in a World War II movie sneaking past the door of the dozing guard on their way to destroy the Nazi headquarters. Sometimes Becker thought that being caught by Milt Silvers was worse than being caught by the Nazis. Silvers saw himself as someone people would describe as "a real character." He collected eccentricities relentlessly. He lived in a converted tugboat under the Brooklyn Bridge and always drove some exotic vehicle like a surplus British army half-track. Becker couldn't remember a time when Milt Silvers owned an ordinary automobile or had a pet more conventional than an iguana. At any opportunity—Rocco Popolizio's phoning on the transparent pretext of checking the accuracy of the interoffice telephone directory, for instance—Silvers would describe every detail of his latest acquisition, speaking in a toneless, mildly nasal voice. Wolferman often compared him to "one of those people who can speak eight languages and can bore the eyeballs out of your head in all eight."

They went into the copy room—all of them glancing automatically toward the Bombshell's chair, which turned out to be unoccupied—and crossed through the freight elevator passage between the copy room and the photo lab. They made their way through the photo lab, drawing a few curious stares, and eventually emerged in the hall right in front of the main bank of elevators. "Brilliant!" Wolferman said.

An elevator on its way up rather than down stopped almost immediately, the door opened, and Milt Silvers walked out. "I've been in Queens," he said, although nobody had asked. "I got a deal on an old London taxi." The elevator door shut. No other elevator doors opened. "It's going to be a big change from that John Deere tractor I've been driving," Silvers went on. "But, to tell you the truth, parking a tractor in Manhattan has gotten to be a real hassle. People always have some smart remark about the price of soybeans, of course. I remember a couple of months ago, I drove up to '21' in my tractor, and I thought the doorman's eyes. . . ."

Becker had found that he was able to tune Silvers out by employing some methods of concentration he had picked up while doing a Business story on a Thai mystic who was also a plastics tycoon. He had already heard the "21" story, which had a punch line something like "Well, I'll be" or "I sure never saw anything like that in midtown Manhattan before."

The bell signaling an arriving elevator—down this time—brought Becker out of his trance.

"You fellows going to lunch?" Silvers said.

"Flu shots," Wolferman said, almost too quickly, as he led the group into the elevator. "We decided to go together to buck each other up."

"I'll never forget what they said down in medical when I asked them about shots for my alligator, Iago," Silvers said. "You should have seen the look. . . ."

The elevator had closed. They were away. Without exchanging a word, they walked two blocks downtown, turned right, and entered a Chinese restaurant called the Bamboo Gardens. As they entered, Wolferman held up four fingers, and by the time they had settled into their usual booth the bartender was pouring out four martinis. The choice of the Bamboo Gardens as their regular luncheon spot had nothing to do with the food it served; when asked about its specialty, Wolferman always said, "The specialty of the Bamboo Gardens is being two blocks away." Perhaps because proximity was the only compliment ever given its chef, the Bamboo Gardens was never crowded. Its bartender not only responded instantly to Wolferman's hand signals, he responded with drinks in descending strength as the workweek progressed. On Mondays and Tuesdays, when the writers did little beyond sending queries to the bureaus and waiting around for the correspondents to file reports, four fingers meant four martinis. On Wednesdays and Thursdays, when the writers actually wrote, it meant white wine spritzers or even (if done left-handed) plain club soda. By Friday, when going over the stories with the researchers responsible for checking the accuracy of each fact required patience but no close concentration, they had bounced back up to Scotch.

"I heard today that Woody'll be leaving before the end of the year," Wolferman said, when the drinks had been delivered.

"Who told you that?" Becker asked.

"Rocco told me. When he called from the track to say he was out sick."

Everyone at the table looked impressed. Rocco Popolizio had a reputation as a reliable source for office gossip. "Rocco knows a lot," Charlie Sayler said. "Except about horses."

"I'll hate to see Woody go, in a way," Wolferman said. "Not that I've ever understood what he's doing there in the first place."

"He's Ted Towndsend's link to human beings," Murray said. Among the magazine's writers, it was taken for granted that Woody Fenton owed his position at least partly to his friendship, dating back to college, with the magazine's owner—Edward R. Towndsend, an eccentric, rather reclusive coal-and-steel heir whose political views, as far as anyone could tell, consisted totally of a passionate commitment to wild animals. Towndsend made public statements only as the board chairman of an international animal preservation organization called the Springbok Society. It was assumed, though, that he had some non-animal-world opinions that he expected to see reflected in the magazine, and that his old college friend Woody Fenton knew what they were—giving Fenton the sort of power that once accrued to the one man in the native village who could speak English well enough to communicate with the colonial district commissioner.

"I'll be sorry to see him go," Becker said. Becker thought of Woody Fenton—amiable, opaque, golly-ridden—as his protection from the calculating personnel-management schemes of Ralph Holbrook, Syracuse Smiley.

"It looks bad," Charlie Sayler said—speaking in the monotone Wolferman had once compared to the voice used by the airline representative to read the names of passengers who had definitely been aboard the overdue jet. "When all is said and done, you have to say this on behalf of Woody Fenton: he's not overtly harmful."

"I can't believe they'd give it to Smiley," Murray said.

"Believe it," Sayler said. "It's going to be us against him. One smile versus eighty-nine sneers, forever and ever."

It occurred to Becker that most of the people at the table—and most of the writers he regularly had lunch or a drink with during the workweek—did not really think in terms of being at the magazine forever and ever. Even those who were not trying to maneuver themselves into position to be tapped by the golden claw tended to use whatever extra energy they had in ways that had nothing to do with rising in the firm. Their view of the firm always reflected a mild disaffection which Wolferman had once described as resembling the attitude of "enlisted men from Princeton." Charlie Sayler wrote short stories—bleak tales that often seemed to be set in hospitals or old-age homes. Andy Wolferman turned out teenage sports novels—what he called his Jockstraps for Jesus series. Bryan Murray, scrambling cheerfully to support the uncountable horde he had fathered, was working on not just *This Dance Is Mine* but also a food conglomerate's annual report, two freelance pieces for an outdoors magazine, and a thriller based on the murder of someone like Ralph Holbrook and called *Death with a Smile.* Only Charlie Sayler ever spoke of a future that included the magazine. "We'll each get a gold watch from Syracuse Smiley at the end," he often said. "A gold watch and a smile."

"He's never been a reporter, don't forget," Murray said.

"Well, there was that brilliant reporting job he did in France," Wolferman said. Holbrook, as an assistant managing editor on a sort of inspection tour of European bureaus, had arrived for his first visit to Paris late one night and had sent back a cable the following morning that began, "The mood of the people of France is. . . ." A number of writers had pinned it on their office walls next to Holbrook's memo urging restraint in decoration.

"They'd never give it to someone who's never been a reporter," Murray said. "Don't forget how he got into this miserable game."

"I've never known whether to believe that story," Sayler said.

"No doubt about that story," Murray said. "Checked out. Double checked. The city editor of the Syracuse paper read one of those business course books that said an executive was someone who had at least four assistants, and this poor bastard had only three. So he hired Smiley."

Everyone at the table drank in silence for a while.

"He's good on animals," somebody said.

"First-rate on animals."

"A real animal lover."

"The springboks of the world would be safe with old Syracuse Smiley in the saddle."

Becker had written several wild-animal stories himself. The proprietor's interest in the beasts of the field was a standing joke at the magazine, so that any mention of an animal preservation story at a story conference attended by, say, Wolferman or Murray, would result in a burst of mock parrot calls and whistles: "Spring-BOK, spring-BOK, spring-BOK. B'rack, B'rack. Teddy want a springbok.

Spring-BOK." Among the editors, Holbrook alone insisted on going along with the pretext that a story on, say, the threat to the New Brunswick porcupine was being run because "we haven't done wild animals for a while, and this one sounds pretty important." When a story on the international meeting of the Springbok Society had been suggested in Foreign Affairs during a week when Becker was assigned to the section and the Greeks and Turks were having a particularly hard time of it in Cyprus, Howard Fox, the senior editor in charge, had responded to the whistles and calls of "Spring-BOK" by saying, "I think we'll put this Springbok Society story on the list. The alternative is a piece I'd hate to see us run—a distinguished senior editor dismissed from his job at a national newsmagazine in late middle age. Forced to borrow from his dreadful in-laws to pay his children's college tuition. Despondent and possibly suicidal. Spring-BOK. Spring-BOK."

"I just can't believe they'd do it," Murray said.

"A gold watch and a quick smile," Sayler said.

"Why don't you ever run into him and Towndsend's wife playing kissy-face somewhere, Andy?" Murray asked.

"I don't think Towndsend has a wife," Becker said.

"Strictly an animal man," Sayler said.

"If I ever did happen to run across Smiley nuzzling somebody somewhere," Wolferman said, "I want you to know that I would sacrifice a painfully built reputation for nearly awesome discretion to spread it around like a bandit."

"He must be with somebody," Murray said. "Dorothy Matteson told me that when he was sitting in for Woody a couple of months ago he literally chased her around the desk. He would have caught her going around an ordinary-sized desk, but apparently he got winded."

"Smiley can't do the distances," Wolferman said.

"I just can't believe they'd do it," Murray repeated.

The group fell silent. "You're all obviously very sorry now that you gave absolutely no support to my brilliant rhinoceros-head caper," Wolferman said. "There must be a lot of regrets around this table that a truly inspired conspiracy had to be abandoned because the people who could have carried it off were cripped by cowardice and ennui and a pisherkeh world-view."

The others shook their heads. "No regrets," Murray said. On Edward Towndsend's infrequent trips to the city, it was his custom to drop into the offices of the magazine's four or five top editors for what amounted to courtesy calls. A Bamboo Gardens lunch had once been enlivened by antic fantasies about somehow mounting the head of a white rhinoceros—a species not only endangered but huge—on the wall of Ralph Holbrook's office just before Towndsend entered. Three weeks after the conversation, when everyone else had pretty much forgotten about it, Wolferman arrived at lunch with a detailed plan that ran fourteen pages, not counting diagrams.

"We could have saved ourselves," Wolferman said.

"It was overcomplicated, Andy," Becker said. "We never could have pulled it off."

"I think I could have gone along with it if it hadn't included the break-in at the American Museum of Natural History," Murray said.

Wolferman turned to Sayler. "What'd you really think of that plan, Charlie? In your heart of hearts."

Sayler stirred his drink for a moment or two. "Cocka-mamie is the word that leaps to mind," he said.

Wolferman sighed. Then he pulled a piece of copy paper and a pencil out of his pocket. "How about two thirty-three's, a mu-shu, a nineteen, fried dumplings, and the worst hot-and-sour soup in the Greater New York area?" he asked. Everybody nodded. Wolferman wrote some numbers on the copy paper and held it above his head. Then, with the other hand, he held up four fingers.

10 After lunch, Pam Robinson phoned to tell Becker that he might escape a week of innards in the Medicine section. Doc Kennedy seemed to be pulling himself together. "He's down to one thermometer," she said. "I think he's got a good chance of making it through the week if he just gets over the idea that he might have narcolepsy."

"Isn't that a disease that causes people to fall asleep suddenly?"

"That's it," Pam said. "Last week, I'd go into his office and find him snoring over his typewriter. He was sure he had narcolepsy, although it was months ago that we did the piece on it."

"Maybe it has a long incubation period."

"Maybe. Anyway, I think I've convinced him that he was just sleepy from having stayed up all night worrying about having narcolepsy."

Becker went over copies of the queries Carol Goodenow had sent to the bureaus outlining what Lifestyle would need to know for the stories it had scheduled. There were two queries on the two-thirds stocking story. One went to Los Angeles, the bureau that had sent in the suggestion: "Lifestyle scheduling your two-thirds stocking story. Need interview with designer who invented two-thirds look, plus background on him or her. Is he or she the only one doing two-thirds? Where did he or she get the idea? Do two-thirds stockings go two-thirds of the way to knee or two-thirds up leg or what? Does he or she wear stockings his or herself? Or what? Also need examples of film colony two-thirds stocking wearers, etc. Regards, Goodenow." The other query was a "roundup" sent to half a dozen bureaus in the United States and to eight or ten part-time stringers in cities where the magazine did not have a bureau. It said, "Lifestyle scheduling fashion piece on new trend of two-thirds stockings. Has two-thirds stocking rage hit your area? Are pacesetters wearing them or what? Do they go two-thirds up to the knee or two thirds up the leg? Or what? Regards, Goodenow."

Becker picked up the queries and walked across the hall into Carol Goodenow's office. Carol was at her desk, working in one of her pattern-of-discrimination reports to Woody Fenton—monthly reports that outlined just how the management of the magazine was discriminating against women or against one minority or another. Carol's reports were known around the magazine as models of advocacy prose—clear, strong, solidly researched. Andy Wolferman often remarked that they were better than anything that actually appeared in the magazine. Becker always found it amazing that they came from the same young woman who blushed at mildly off-color jokes in story conferences and often burst into tears during disagreements over fact-checking at the end of the week. Carol was bent over her report, carefully making some pencil changes. She looked very serious. She almost always looked serious. She had dark brown eyes and a manner of concentrating them intently on anybody she was talking to. Once or twice, Becker had thought about asking her out to dinner, but he had worried that she might either blush and leave the room or call him a male oppressor and tell him to mind his own business. "Carol," he said.

She looked up from her report. "I put the stocking queries on your desk," she said. "The other ones are still in the cable room."

"Yeah, they're just fine, Carol. Really good. There's just one little thing I wanted to ask you about."

"Yes?"

Was her lower lip starting to quiver? Becker couldn't be certain. He proceeded slowly. "The queries are just fine, Carol. Very thorough. Clear. Couldn't be better. It's just that, well, I was sort of under the impression that, well, that Pete decided not to put that story on the list." Now her lip was definitely quivering.

"Oh no!" she said. She reached for the clipboard she had used in the story conference, flipped through it, and then sank back in her desk chair.

"Well, look, Carol—"

"I don't know what I could have been thinking of. You're absolutely right. It definitely wasn't scheduled."

"Well, Carol, look at it this way," Becker said. "I'm sure it's not a bad story, and we are about due for a stocking story. We haven't done stockings in a really long time."

"I'll have to send out a correction right away."

"Well, what I was thinking, Carol, is that we could

just go ahead as if Pete had put it on the list. I think Genine and I can figure out some way to sneak it on by the end of the week. Everyone else'll think Pete changed his mind, and he'll never know the difference. Listen, Pete probably doesn't remember what he had for lunch an hour ago. I think we should just go ahead with it."

"Do you really think it's O.K.?"

"Carol," Becker said, "do you actually think there's a trend for wearing two-thirds of a stocking in Los Angeles?"

"Not really," she said. "I figured that Sicola in Los Angeles hadn't sent in any back-of-the-book suggestions for a while and was getting some pressure from Barnett out there and has a girlfriend who wears two-thirds stockings, or would if there were any, and made the suggestion."

"Exactly the way I figured it," Becker said. "So here's what will happen—the same thing that happened during that last yo-yo revival, when Smithers saw one of his yo-yo nephews with a yo-yo and decided the yo-yo was making a comeback. We send the queries on two-thirds stockings to the bureaus and the stringers. The junior guy at the bureau will get the query and, trying to show what a tiger he is, he'll find some people wearing two-thirds stockings or he'll invent a couple to keep the bureau chief happy. Sicola, I assure you, will come up with a designer who thinks two-thirds stockings are absolutely the latest thing and who'll take credit for having invented them. The stringers are paid by the word, and you can't write many words about not being able to find any two-thirds stockings. So they'll find some. Then we'll take all of those reports and write a nice little fifty-liner out of them, and people will read it, and then people will start wearing two-thirds stockings. So everything will be just as we said it was."

Carol Goodenow tapped her pencil on the desk for a moment or two. Then she stuck out her hand for Becker to shake. "Done," she said.

Back in his own office, feeling pleased that the two-thirds stockings matter had been worked out so easily, Becker could see the White House Cabinet Room again. The President is entering now, apparently having timed his entrance to take place just after the Secretary of State said, "Gentlemen, the President's wife is pregnant." The President looks a bit worried or perhaps a bit self-satisfied, or perhaps both. When the President enters, everyone stands. It is obvious that they are unsure how to react. Should there be congratulations? Is he expecting condolences? Will the President treat his wife's condition like any other crisis that might have necessitated a special meeting of the cabinet—asking the CIA director for his long-range prediction and turning to the Army Chief of Staff for a report on how much firepower is in the area? The cabinet secretaries and generals and National Security Council people and White House aides glance around at one another in an effort to divine what sort of response is proper. The Secretary of State is presumably in the best position to know—he must have spoken to the President about making the announcement—but no one can see the Secretary of State's expression. He has turned toward the door to greet the President. He is visible only from the rear—the back of his elegantly cut pinstriped suit, the back of his carefully trimmed gray hair. The only person in the room who seems to have no doubt about how he should react is the Secretary of Labor, an alternately gruff and hearty man who began his career as a steelworker. "Atta boy, Mr. President," the Secretary of Labor says, winking and elbowing the person next to him—

the scholarly, rather stiff Secretary of the Treasury—in the ribs. "Atta way to go."

The Cabinet Room faded from Becker's mind. He sat at his desk and tried to think logically about whether the pregnancy of the President's wife was fact or fiction. If Wentzell had been telling the truth, and the President planned to risk a secret abortion, there was obviously some time limit within which he had to act. But what was it? Becker realized that he knew very little about pregnancy. His wife, Greta, had never been pregnant. He had wanted to have children, but the year or two during which he and Greta had any reason to believe that the marriage was going to last happened to coincide with her most intense period of environmentalism. During that period, she thought about children strictly in terms of how much of the world's limited supply of nonrenewable fossil fuels each of them would use. When she saw a large family taking a Sunday stroll, she would sometimes shudder visibly, and mutter to Becker something like, "selfish pigs." She constantly pressed him for the true number of children Bryan Murray had, and when he insisted he didn't know she accused him of participating in a "gigantic cover-up." Just before Greta became an environmentalist, there had been a few months during which they might have thought about children, but at that time she was intensely opposed to the Vietnam War—she used to berate the postman for continuing to work for war criminals—and she kept saying that she would not bear sons to murder or be murdered on the battlefield. Becker had tried briefly to convince her that the war was bound to be over by the time any child they might have reached draft age, but then he gave up.

Becker tried to remember whether he had learned anything at all about pregnancy from the stories he had written. As a back-of-the-book floater, he had accumulated a store of knowledge on all sorts of subjects—a knowledge of millenarian sects from his bondage in Religion, familiarity with the workings of hot-air balloons from a summer week in Sports, more than he wanted to know about New Math from a period spent in Education when Milt Silvers went to the hospital with an alligator bite. One of the problems with a floater's knowledge, though, was its spottiness. He knew a lot about millenarian sects, but he had no idea what, say, Methodists believe. From several weeks in the Business section at one time or another, he happened to have learned a lot about Asian currency manipulation and the speculative market in bull semen, but he wouldn't have had the first notion about how to go about obtaining a mortgage. He knew practically nothing about French impressionism, but he could have delivered an after-dinner speech on the work of one abstract expressionist who happened to die when the regular Art writer was on vacation.

The one story he could remember having written on anything to do with childbirth had given him his usual rather narrow view of the subject. It was about an obstetrician, named Emmanual Froelich, who was also an amateur racing driver. Froelich had been accused of endangering his patients by inducing births on Tuesdays, Wednesdays, and Thursdays so as to be available for weekend races. The story had been carefully checked for accuracy by Pam Robinson and cleared by the magazine's libel lawyer. Many of the accusations reported in it, in fact, had already appeared, unchallenged, in a medical newsletter.

Froelich, it was thought, would not have sued except for the wording of what was called around the magazine the "drop head"—to distinguish it from the "subject head," which in this case said "Obstetrics." Drops eventually came across the desk of Ralph Holbrook, who took some pride in changing almost every one he encountered. For the Froelich drop, Holbrook had settled on the nickname given to Froelich by some of the delivery room nurses—"Middle of the Week Manny." Froelich sued for six hundred thousand dollars, which, perhaps by coincidence, was what he himself was being sued for by some patients charging malpractice.

The magazine's lawyers tried to argue that Froelich was a public figure—therefore not capable of being libeled unless malice could be shown—because of his car-racing career and the fact that, as the NewsPeople section would have put it, his name had once been "linked" to that of a disco owner of noble birth. After the suit became public, the tabloids began referring to him in headlines as "Disco Doc"—although one of the first matters he testified to by deposition was that he had never been inside a disco and that the "intimate relationship" he had been accused of having with the disco proprietor had been strictly professional.

For reasons known only to the lawyers involved, Becker was required to be present throughout the trial, even though he testified only briefly. Once or twice, he went from court to the magazine for a late afternoon drink with Wolferman, who berated him for having the good fortune to be assigned to sit around a courthouse all day. "It's like a combat infantryman getting temporary duty to escort a body to Hawaii," Wolferman said. "It's a shocking boondoggle, and I'm the one who should be doing the doggling.

This Froelich business was a Sports story that was stolen by Medicine. The guy's a racing driver. Most of the people who were suing him were probably knocked up by golfers or tennis players or at least bowlers. Also, I resent your representing us as a slanderer. I'm much more slanderous than you are. I would have had the guy pulling out babies when he was too drunk to see whether it was a boy or a girl. I would have had him diddling the nurses, diddling the patients, diddling the patients' husbands, diddling the other doctors, diddling the Blue Cross inspector. I would have really let the son of a bitch have it, instead of writing some pisherkeh little piece about having babies on Thursday instead of Friday. I would have been in court for a year and a half. The trouble is that nobody takes Sports seriously, not even the goyim. That's my cross."

Becker had expected Dr. Froelich to be a dashing type, but the doctor turned out to be an unimposing-looking man—short, soft-spoken, with a fringe of gray hair and heavy glasses. Becker, to his surprise, rather liked him. They spent a lot of time talking together while the lawyers were in seemingly interminable conferences in the judge's chambers. Becker knew a bit about racing—Wolferman happened to be on vacation the week the Sports section scheduled a piece about accusations of sexual activity during pit stops at Sebring—and the doctor found him an appreciative audience for stories about race tactics and gearbox complications. Froelich didn't seem particularly interested in obstetrics. "I happened to have a good pair of hands," he told Becker. "What was I going to be with a good pair of hands—a shortstop?" Toward the end of the trial, they were feeling more like allies than adversaries.

"Can you keep a secret?" Emmanual Froelich asked Becker one day, as they sat together on a hard bench just outside the courtroom. "Aren't journalists supposed to be professionally committed to keeping certain secrets?"

"Well, I'm not exactly in that end of the business—the secret-keeping end," Becker said. "But, sure, I think I can keep a secret."

"My wife is the one who insisted that we sue," Dr. Froelich said. "Because of the headline. I didn't want to sue. No matter which way it comes out, I'm going to miss two races just because of this trial. Also, the story in your magazine didn't damage my practice. In fact, it brought me a lot of patients. You know how some women are about their obstetricians and gynecologists. The minute they heard I was the Disco Doc, the racing driver, they flocked to my office. They expected to find the Marquis de Portago, I guess, and maybe get a few juicy tidbits about this supposed affair with that dreadful woman from the discotheque. They were a little disappointed in that regard, of course, but most of them remained patients. I actually am a pretty good doctor. I say that without egotism. Is it the shortstop's fault, after all, that he was born with quick hands?"

"Well, Doctor, I kind of figured your wife might have had something to do with it," Becker said. "People's wives often get upset about what's in print. They have a lot of loyalty, and all that." Becker was attempting to be diplomatic. He had seen Froelich's wife in court several times—an imperious woman who would sweep in, sit in the front row for a while with a stern look on her face, like someone who had the unpleasant duty of inspecting the progress the serfs were making on the back garden, and then sweep out again.

After Becker had observed Mrs. Froelich for a while, he began to regret that the doctor's relationship with the disco proprietor had been only professional.

"That's not the secret," Dr. Froelich said.

"What?"

"What I just told you—that I sued at the insistence of my wife—is not the secret I asked if you could keep."

"Oh," Becker said, somewhat puzzled. They sat in silence for a while. Occasionally, someone would pass them on the way to get salted peanuts or peanut-butter crackers from a vending machine next to the elevator. Becker didn't know whether he was supposed to ask what the secret really was. How did reporters handle such situations? Did they tell anecdotes of their own to lead the other person on? Did they bully reluctant sources? During his tenure in the Washington bureau, Becker knew that the State Department desk men and Commerce Department press officers were telling him only the lies they were instructed to tell all reporters. It had seemed pointless to ask for some special little lie they had told no one else.

"Do you want to know the secret?" Dr. Froelich finally asked.

"Oh, yes," Becker blurted out—and then, fearing that he might have seemed too eager, added, "If you'd like to tell me." Becker was becoming seriously interested in the secret. He wondered if Dr. Froelich was going to say that all of the charges about inducing labor were true. Or perhaps that the charges didn't go far enough. Maybe someone had been seriously injured. Maybe, as Wolferman had imagined, Dr. Froelich was diddling the nurses or even the Blue Cross inspector.

"The secret is that my wife had no objection to the part about the middle of the week," Dr. Froelich said. "There's nothing wrong with that. Who wants to be born on a weekend? Half the stores are closed. The restaurants are crowded. It's hard to get a taxi. No, no. She didn't mind that. Here's what she minded about my being called 'Middle of the Week Manny' in a national magazine, and this is the secret." Froelich paused, and then continued in a lower voice. "She hates it when people call me Manny. She considers it an undignified name. She always calls me Emmanual. She spent years making me Emmanual, and it was ruined in one headline. There you have it, young man."

"You mean you're missing those races just for that?" Becker said.

Froelich nodded, and smiled.

"Listen, I'm sorry about all of this," Becker said. "I didn't write the headline, but I did use that name in the story. I'm really sorry to have caused you any trouble."

"Please," Froelich said, holding up his hand. "Don't give it another thought. In the first place, it was truly the headline that angered her, not the story. Also, you were simply doing your job. It sounds like a most interesting job—a new subject every week. New stories. Nothing like an unbroken string of pulling out babies. I don't suppose you're required to work on weekends, are you?"

"Not usually, Doctor," Becker said.

"Please," Froelich said, holding up his hand again. "Please. Call me Manny."

The trial had ended in a small out-of-court settlement. Whatever Becker learned from it, he thought, as he walked to the window and once again looked down at the intersection below, had nothing to do with the medical facts of pregnancy. He didn't know, offhand, when an abortion would no longer be safe or whether the age of the First Lady was a factor. He didn't know when the First Lady would, as his mother always put it, "start to show." Whether he planned to investigate the subject for the purposes of writing fact or fiction, he would need some simple background—the sort of background he acquired quickly, two or three times a week, when a researcher walked in with a file folder containing what he needed to know about the recent history of Syria or what art critics had said over the years about a recently deceased abstract expressionist.

11 Becker got off the IRT subway at the Eighteenth Street station. His rent-controlled apartment—once his occupation, still his most cherished possession—was only two blocks away, on Sixteenth and Seventh Avenue. Although the traditional northern boundary of Greenwich Village was Fourteenth, both Becker and his landlord had a view of the Village broad enough to encompass Sixteenth Street. The landlord liked to talk about how much he could be getting for a one-bedroom apartment "in the heart of the Village" if it were not for the vicious inequities of the rent control laws. Becker had not lost his feeling of identification with the Midwesterners who had come to the Village in *Wonderful Town*—one of whom he had played in a college production. Becker was always pleased to look out the train window and see "18 St"—although graffiti had made it rather difficult to make out. It occurred to him that someone turning up an important Washington story might be rewarded with an assignment to a foreign bureau—some snazzy, graffiti-less European capital where a newsmagazine correspondent could live in relative splendor because of the tax laws and an ex-

pense account and some little-known wrinkle in the currency exchange system and a housing allowance from Max Eisen so generous that Andy Wolferman's response to seeing any particularly opulent mansion in a foreign capital was to say, "It's either an Arab embassy or the home of our bureau chief." As it happened, though, he liked living in Manhattan. He did not even mind living in a city where everything seemed covered by graffiti, he realized as he walked up the steps and out of the station, although during a week he spent in the Behavior section writing a story on "street sociology," he found himself mildly depressed at the thought of living in a city where so many people seemed to be able to get grants to study the literary and sociological meaning of the graffiti.

Sometimes, as he walked from the subway to his apartment after a day of writing, he found that his mind translated everything in the neighborhood into a newsmagazine story—a Business story about Levy's Laundromat ("When Nathan Levy first installed his washing machines in a storefront on Seventh Avenue, in 1952, the prospects for an alliterative Jewish laundromat in the northern part of Greenwich Village seemed dim. . . ."), a Medicine story about the storefront office of Salvador & Salvador ("Last week, thanks to the efforts of a pioneering couple in Manhattan's North Village, there seemed to be evidence for the first time that a combination of chiropractic and clairvoyance could go a long way toward curing the common cold. . . .), an Entertainment Arts story about the rather drab line of red brick, four-story buildings that held his rent-controlled apartment ("One of the most extensive talent searches in Hollywood history finally ended last week when Columbia announced that a non-actor who owns four buildings in Manhattan's Greenwich Village had been chosen to play the rapacious landlord in the forthcoming *No Hot Water*. . . ."). As he approached his own building, Becker saw a bulky figure reclining on the front stoop. It was Leonard Wentzell.

"Pal of my youth," Wentzell said in greeting.

Becker sat down on the stoop. "I didn't expect to see you in New York so soon," he said.

"I had a little project," Wentzell said. "So I thought I'd drop by to say hello. It's been a while."

"Almost a full day."

"Still in Lifestyle?"

"Still there."

"Isn't Lifestyle where you were going to run that story I gave you about the latest thing among the poofters in Akron?"

"I couldn't seem to interest them in that one," said Becker, who had, in fact, not had the nerve to bring it up.

"All that gay stuff is very big these days," Wentzell said. "Gay activists, the International Violet Conspiracy, all that. I would have thought they would jump at that Akron story. A little slice of life was what it was."

"Pete Smithers is the senior editor for Lifetyle, and he gets very pissed off when the subject comes up," Becker said. "I wouldn't want to bring up anything like that while he's there. He might have a heart attack."

"Is Smithers the dumb one you told me about—with his feet on the desk?"

"That's him," Becker said. He told Wentzell a couple of new Smithers anecdotes—Smithers misunderstanding a story on American economic history because he was under the impression that Thorst and Veblen were two people who had written a textbook together, Carol Goodenow's lodging an official protest with management after Smithers had referred to Joan of Arc as "that nutty French dike."

Wentzell hauled himself to his feet and made a pass at straightening his suit. "I have to run," he said. "The person expects me."

"Can't I get you a drink?"

Wentzell shook his head and then, tapping himself a couple of times on the temple, said, "Have to stay alert for this one." He turned to walk away. Then, as if in afterthought, he said, "It might be a good idea if you gave Mary Jane Wheeler a call."

"Our Mary Jane Wheeler? Mary Jane Wheeler from home?"

"Who else's Mary Jane Wheeler?"

"Is this 'little project' you're on sponsored by my mother or something—'What Freddy needs at this time in his life is to start seeing some real nice girl from home'?"

Wentzell shook his head. He glanced up and down Sixteenth Street. "What I think you should call her about," he said, in a voice Becker could hardly hear, "is the matter we discussed in Washington last night. I had a feeling when you left that, despite our long friendship and the many tidbits I've managed to pass your way, you might feel a little more comfortable with this one if you had some confirmation."

"And I can get confirmation by calling Mary Jane Wheeler in Nebraska?"

"Mary Jane Wheeler in Washington," Wentzell said.

"Mary Jane Wheeler, Freddy, is a special assistant to the President. Liaison to starving artists and Mau-Maus and just about anybody else who can be shown to have no power whatsoever—but, Freddy, companion of my golden youth, she is also trusted confidante to the prime tree-planter herself."

"Our Mary Jane Wheeler!"

"Our very own," Wentzell said. "Listen, Freddy. Pal. I don't want you to spend the rest of your life writing about hula hoops and all that dreck. This is the chance of a lifetime. You may get rich. You may get famous. You may get to be the managing editor so you can tell this shmuck to get his feet off the furniture. You don't want to be rich and famous? You don't want to be introduced to girls with big boobs at cocktail parties as Fred Becker the Investigative Reporter? You don't want to be able to tell what's-his-name—Rochester Smarmy—to stick it in his ear?"

"Syracuse Smiley," Becker said.

Wentzell looked at his watch. "I've got to get going," he said. "These kind of people don't like to be kept waiting, if you know what I mean. I'll be in touch."

Wentzell walked down Sixteenth Street. Two or three doors down the street, a super nodded as he passed—probably assuming that he was one of the gypsy card-readers from around the corner. Becker remained on the stoop, thinking about the possibility of calling Mary Jane Wheeler in Washington.

Could anyone they had known as children in Omaha really be in a position to know the truth about some nationally significant bit of gynecology? Just accepting the fact that somebody he had grown up with was a special assistant to the President required a leap of imagination for Becker. He wasn't sure that he was ready to have people from his calculus class occupying positions of responsibility.

It was not that having contemporaries in responsible positions made him feel old or made him feel that his own career was not moving along fast enough. He had not thought of what he did for a living as a career since the day Syd Berg pointed out the failure of his voice to carry as far as the cleaning lady dusting the fourteenth row. It was simply that he had a lot more confidence in people who held responsible positions in government and industry before responsible positions in government and industry began to be held by people he knew. The latest example had been provided by Roger Hawkinson. A few weeks before, Becker's mother had written to say that Roger Hawkinson had been named American ambassador to some middle-sized oil sheikdom in the Persian Gulf—a place run by a feudal monarch whose name Becker could never get straight during stints in the Foreign Affairs section, since the name that kept running through his mind was the Abu of Exxon. Roger Hawkinson had been a spoiled kid of such predictable tantrums that Becker knew him to be a cliché even before he knew the word. Once, Roger Hawkinson had actually taken his bat and ball and gone home because he wasn't allowed to play first base.

"Nobody does that except in the comics," Becker remembered saying as Roger collected his equipment, putting the baseball back into a cardboard box that only a true creep would have thought to keep. For a moment, the comic-book aspect of what Roger Hawkinson was doing upset Becker. Was he going to begin seeing sailors whose biceps popped into a ball after every can of spinach? Would there be fights in which the loser got thrown through the swinging doors of the bar onto the sidewalk?

Roger had turned to him sternly, pursing his lips in a way that Becker later recalled as having caused him to resemble Thomas E. Dewey at thirteen. "Pig fart," Hawkinson said. Becker didn't know whether it was meant as a simple expletive—as in "Oh, pig fart"—or if Roger was calling him a pig fart, in which case he would probably have to fight him. He had no precedent to help in his decision: it was the first time he had ever heard the term. He was never to know. Roger Hawkinson said "pig fart" once again and then, without waiting for a response, ran home.

"This means a forfeit," Leonard Wentzell had shouted after him. Wentzell constantly warned of forfeit—also balks. Forfeits and balks were his specialty. He was an awkward player, but he was always among the first four or five boys to be chosen—strictly because of his arguing and heckling ability. The notion of a forfeit was, of course, meaningless in a pickup game. Still, Wentzell made forfeit sound like a fate to be avoided at any cost. His cry of "balk!" carried even more dread. As far as Becker could remember, nobody was ever sent to first base on a balk during their entire childhood, but a lot of pitchers were thrown off their stride when that awful word was screeched from the sidelines by Wentzell, who could make it sound like some horrible perversity.

How could American interests in the Persian Gulf be protected by a little creep like Roger Hawkinson, Becker wondered. Roger Hawkinson was a pig fart. If the Abu of

Exxon said something Roger didn't like during a negotiating session, Roger would be likely to pick up his portfolio and go home. One of the reasons Becker could never get excited about who won which political campaign was that he suspected that in some town somewhere in the United States there were people who knew the winner to be a spoiled little pig fart.

But Mary Jane Wheeler had never taken her bat and ball and gone home just because she wasn't allowed to play first base. Being a girl, Mary Jane Wheeler wasn't allowed to play at all. There was no reason to suspect her. As far as Becker could remember, she had never exhibited any pig-fart tendencies. In fact, the only tendency he could remember her exhibiting was a tendency toward bustiness. She had been the president of the Junior Red Cross chapter, he remembered for some reason, and a judge of the student court and maybe recording secretary of the Honor Society. Something in the Honor Society. Becker, after not having seen her for fifteen years, still thought of her as trustworthy. If he asked her about the condition of the President's wife, she would either tell him or tell him honestly that she couldn't tell him—which, under the circumstances, amounted to the same thing. By phoning Mary Jane Wheeler, Becker would probably be able to find out whether the First Lady's pregnancy was fact or fiction. He wasn't certain that he was ready to know.

Tuesday

12 "Well, what have we got so far, Jack?" Woody Fenton said, puffing on his pipe. Jack Thompson, Max Eisen, and Ralph Holbrook were again gathered around his desk.

"Well, we've still got the secretary of state on the cover," Thompson said, automatically raising his voice a bit to carry over the expanse of blond wood between him and the managing editor.

"Right. Good. Swell guy. Did I ever tell you what he told me about what the prime minister of Portugal was doing in his private office on weekends, right when Scott was filing all that stuff about what a great reformer this guy is and how he's the hope of Portugal?"

"No, you never did, Woody."

"Wow!" Fenton said. "Golly!" He shook his head in wonderment at the thought of it. "What else we got?"

"Well, we may have a little war on our hands."

Fenton looked at Max Eisen, who shrugged, and said, "I'm afraid it's escaped my attention, but there're so many these days that we do tend to miss one now and then."

"Not that kind of war," Thompson went on.

"Smithers and Venery are fighting about whether that sex change capital story is Lifestyle or Medicine. If we decide on Medicine, that means putting off the pancreas for a while, because next week we're locked in with the color pages on loop colostomies."

"What do you think, Max?" Fenton asked the chief of correspondents.

"I think Smithers and Venery are both hoping to brighten up their week with a lot of reports from Indiana on sex change operations—maybe even with some pictures."

"We've held the pancreas for a long time," Holbrook said. "It's in danger of getting a bit stale."

"The reports from Indiana point to Medicine," Eisen said. "It's basically about the doctor and this operation and all these private parts coming unglued." Eisen could usually be counted on to take a position opposing the one taken by Ralph Holbrook. He had occasionally been toasted at the Bamboo Gardens with the words "Anybody who hates Syracuse Smiley and travels first class can't be all bad."

"De Bakey's a hell of a doctor," Fenton said.

"No doubt about that, Woody," Holbrook said.

"He's no slouch—De Bakey," Thompson said.

"Remember when he was here for lunch?" Fenton said. "The way he sliced his steak?"

"The man knows how to use a knife, no doubt about that," Holbrook said.

"I used to love the emergency room when I was a young police reporter," Fenton said.

"I know what you mean," Eisen said.

"All that shouting. All that blood. 'Nurse, where is this patient's arm?' I heard an intern say that once: 'Nurse, where is this patient's arm?' Nothing like it. What experience! Golly! Learned more there than you can learn in ten years as an editor."

"You're right about that," Eisen said. "No substitute for reporting."

Holbrook turned his pipe around and knocked it sharply three or four times on the arm of his chair—jarring loose some old tobacco or calling for attention. "Christian Barnard's good, too," he said.

"Gosh, yes," Fenton said.

The others nodded. Holbrook emitted a sort of echoing gosh. Thompson said, "Just as good, I suppose, in a way."

"Well, it was hard to tell because we had beef stroganoff that day he was here for lunch," Fenton said. "It's not really a dish that lets somebody show what he can do."

"That's true enough," Holbrook said. "A lot of the cutting has been done already."

There was a long pause. "Gosh!" Fenton said again, and the others nodded.

"Then shall I tell them to switch the sex change capital story to Medicine and hold the pancreas?" Thompson asked.

"Fine," Fenton said. "I think that's pretty much the conclusion we've reached. Anything more on that wild monkey story?"

"We're still having trouble getting a man into the jungle there, Woody," Eisen said. "I tried to hire a gunboat, but the deal fell through. If somebody's back there slaughtering wild monkeys, I wish he'd tell us how the hell he got there."

"Well, we might have to write it from the clips," Fenton said.

"We're about due for a wild monkey story," Holbrook said.

"I'd like to be able to tell the President we're running the story when I ask him Thursday why we're not slapping a trade embargo on those fellows for peddling wild monkey skins. If the briefing doesn't get postponed again, of course."

Jack Thompson made a notation on his clipboard. There was silence for a while.

"Fourteen times," Fenton finally said. "Walt Heinlich was down there fourteen times."

13 Fred Becker was sitting behind Roger Burnside's desk, drinking a cup of coffee and reading through the obscene topiary piece that Burnside had written the week before. Smithers wanted it "freshened up a little." As far as the readers of the magazine were concerned, of course, there was nothing stale about the piece as it stood—none of them had seen it—but among senior editors it was considered bad form to run a story left over from the previous week without making some changes. It was as if a story that hadn't run, even for reasons that had nothing to do with its quality, carried with it some malformation that had to be straightened out before it was allowed to be read again by the managing editor. The original story looked fine to Becker, but he knew that one of his jobs early in the week was to change it in some way—if for no other reason than to give Smithers the opportunity to change it back. Nobody had much to do until Wednesday, and any diversion was welcome.

The obscene topiary craze had started at a singles apartment complex in Houston. An electronic software salesman with an artistic flare and a taste for pranks had, in the middle of the night, redone four boxwood bushes next to the swimming pool. At first, the reaction of the apartment complex management had been to threaten the salesman with eviction and to talk about pressing charges for malicious mischief and corrupting the morals of a minor (the minor in question being the manager's nine-year-old son, who came in from an early morning swim and told his mother, "One of the shrubs by the pool has got itself a dingdong."). Then one of the local papers ran a story about the prank, and the singles complex found itself with a waiting list for apartments. Inevitably, some of the other singles buildings in town tried to compete. Soon, the craze had spread to Arizona and erupted in Southern California. Burnside had included a quote from the leader of a human response clinic in Santa Barbara, who said that the obscene topiary movement was a creative merging of people's increasing openness about sex and their increasing openness about the open. There was also a quote from a Baptist minister in Fort Worth, who said that dirty bushes provided the final symbol of the society's decadence. The American Society of Landscape Architects was apparently set to argue out a resolution at its annual general convention—a group of radical landscapers having seized on the issue to "open up some musty minds and shake up the establishmentarians whose idea of something daring is to mix the color of the roses."

Becker changed the quotation about decadence, substituting a similar statement by a Church of Christ minister in Phoenix. He toyed with the lead paragraph a bit. ("At Dallas's swinging Tarzan & Jane Manors apartment complex, there have always been a lot of ideas about what to do late at night in the bushes. One night last month, Lane

Scroggins, a software salesman with hardcore ideas, tossed back a few margaritas and figured out something to do *to* the bushes.") Then Becker added a couple of sentences about the radical caucus of the landscape society, just to make certain Smithers had something to edit out. If a story called for a sentence about people who might be considered offensive by Smithers, Becker always put in three or four sentences— a couple of which almost cried out for Smithers to cross them out while muttering "goddamned hippies" or "the queers are everywhere." It kept him away from the story.

"I trust I'm not disturbing your professional pursuits."

Becker looked up and saw Yitzchak Katz standing before him. Katz was a Hasidic rabbi who often tried to press stories on him when he was doing the Religion section. Before Becker became a floater, he had always assumed that Lifestyle or Entertainment Arts would be the section most heavily bombarded by press agents, but it turned out that Religion was worse than either of them. One brand of Lutherans would phone to report some misdeed of another brand of Lutherans. The press representative of dissident priests would appear to bear witness against the bishop. The public relations man retained by an Episcopal priest who specialized in jazz masses would send letter after letter calling attention to the priest's new book on how to talk to teenagers. The pressure from press agents was one reason Becker started offering up daily prayers to St. Regis (an unworldly scholarship student from the Midwest, Becker had decided, whose martyrdom took the form of being torn apart and possibly cannibalized by a horde of crazed debutantes) for deliverance from Religion. At one point, Becker resorted to an escape method that supposedly had been used successfully some years before by a desperate floater trapped in the Religion section of another newsmagazine: he began putting "alleged" in front of any religious event whose historical authenticity was at all in question—writing about the "alleged discovery of Moses in the bullrushes" or the "alleged resurrection of Jesus Christ." The senior editor for the section, Ed Winstead, simply crossed out "alleged" wherever he found it, without comment. Finally Rob Rowan, looking spent but determined, returned to take up a dreary story list dominated by a disagreement between Methodists and Episcopalians over the issue of apostolic succession.

Rabbi Katz had been one of the most persistent of the Religion story touts. Even more irritating than his persistence was his habit of accusing Becker of failing to run stories about the Smetena Hasidim—a group so obscure that even Rob Rowan had never heard of it—because of "self-hatred."

"But I'm not Jewish," Becker would argue.

"Just as I thought," the rabbi would say. "The worst kind."

Katz spoke with a slight accent, but Becker was virtually certain that he had been born in America. Despite his accent and his beard and his black hat and his side-curls, he failed to look rabbinical. He was a young man, athletically built and over six feet tall. His beard and side-curls were blond. His eyes were blue. His jaw—or what was visible of it behind the beard—was square. The first time Yitzchak Katz materialized in his doorway, Becker had the feeling of staring at a beach boy in a rabbi costume. Andy Wolferman, who wandered in one day when Katz was trying to persuade Becker to run a story on the Smetena rebbe's contention that there was a talmudic injunction against double-decker buses, insisted that he recognized the rabbi as someone he had seen playing intramural rugby at Williams College some years before. "It's the big forward with side-curls added—I swear it," Wolferman had said, but Becker assumed that he meant it as a joke. Becker took Wolferman absolutely seriously only on matters of romantic liaisons and related office gossip.

"Hello, Rabbi Katz," Becker said. "I'm afraid I'm not doing Religion this week. Rob Rowan's been back for some time."

"Yes, I already had a very nice chat with Mr. Rowan. We had a most interesting discussion of the false messiahs of the eighteenth century. Most interesting." Katz smiled what was presumably meant to be a shy, scholarly smile—a smile that on him somehow came out looking like the broad grins Becker had seen on the faces of Four-H boys praised at the Nebraska State Fair for having raised the prize-winning heifer.

"I trust I'm not disturbing you in the course of your professional duties," Katz went on.

"Oh, no, Rabbi, it's not that. It's just that I'm afraid I can't really do much for you this week. I'm in Lifestyle."

"Precisely why I ventured to come to see you," Katz said. "I have some information that might be of some interest to you professionally, if I may take a moment or two of your important time to appraise you of it."

Becker just nodded. Katz was enough trouble in Religion. Was he going to follow Becker all around the magazine—floating just behind the floater like a severe black-white-and-blond kite? Would he have a tip on a soft-ball game between rabbinical seminaries for the Sports section? Would he wander in while Becker was doing Medicine and offer him first crack at a story about the top circumciser in Brooklyn? Would he be on the phone to the Architecture & Design section whenever Becker was there to propose a piece on new ideas in ritual-bath design? Techniques of Hebrew instruction for Education? Jewish jokes for Entertainment Arts? Becker knew that the wisest course of action would be to discourage Rabbi Katz immediately, but he didn't think he could bear another lecture on self-hatred.

"What'd you have in mind, Rabbi?" he said.

"Kosher fast food."

"Kosher fast food?"

"Precisely," the rabbi said. "It's a natural. Our group, under the leadership of the wise and greatly beloved Rebbe Simchas Golbhelder, is starting a chain. The only question left is the name. We're thinking of Nosh-a-Minute, but there are also those among us who favor Super-Nosh. Naturally, we would be interested in suggestions on that matter from someone of your wide professional experience and background, Mr. Becker. Please do not feel you must limit yourself to names that include the word 'nosh.' In fact, Fress Factory is also a name we have considered."

"But Rabbi, isn't this a little out of your line?" Becker asked. "I mean, I thought your group was interested mainly in studying the Talmud and living a religious life. A fast-food chain?"

"Try to see it our way, Mr. Becker. All of the meshuggeneh sects that try to steal our children are in business. They have restaurants. They have fishing boats. They have begging operations. Are we to stand by helplessly and watch them? No. We have to, as the English saying goes, get into the scrum."

The rugby allusion gave Becker a start. Could Wolferman be right about Katz? A Hasidic rugby player? "Rabbi," he said, rising from his desk, "I think it's a Business story."

"Unfortunately, in the Business section I know nobody, Mr. Becker," Katz said. "You I know. Also, it's a trend. Perhaps a craze. A lifestyle, even."

"I'll bring it up this afternoon to the senior editor, Rabbi," Becker said, moving to the clothes hook to get his sport jacket. "I've got a lunch date now, but I'll certainly mention it to him this afternoon."

"You might mention that the trademark on Nosh-a-Minute has been applied for," Katz said. "I'm sure such a reminder is unnecessary, but you might just mention it, perhaps."

"I'll be sure to mention that," Becker said. He pulled on his jacket and rushed past Katz. "I surely will."

"I hope I haven't disturbed your professional pursuits with these inquiries," Katz said, his voice trailing off as Becker, walking in the heel-and-toe style he had learned while doing a piece on Olympic walkers for the Sports section, reached the elevator, took a quick look around to see if Milt Silvers was lurking nearby, and plunged into an express to the lobby.

He actually did have a luncheon engagement, although he would have invented one to escape from Yitzchak

Katz. His usual uneasiness in Katz's presence had been aggravated by the discussion of restaurants run by religious sects. He had avoided such places partly because he half expected the waitress who shuffled over with the menus to be his ex-wife, Greta, dressed in whatever lunatic costume the sect favored—a sari, maybe, or a long and dirty gingham gown. Until the final letter he had received from her, Greta had still been a militant environmentalist. She had given up using stationery; her letters arrived on increasingly recycled scraps of paper. At first, she just wrote on the back of phone company notices or grocery store flyers. Gradually, though, she began using pieces of paper that some other environmentalist had used for a letter to her—crossing out the previous message or simply writing between the lines without crossing out anything. (Did she intend him to read the previous user's letter, Becker wondered whenever he received one of those, or was she also committed to preserving the world's limited supply of pencil lead?) Some of the paper showed signs not just of having been written on but of having been rained or snowed on. Becker figured that Greta was gathering up some of the paper from camping areas or roadsides—cleaning up the environment at the same time she was protecting the forests from future destruction by the stationery industry. Then, in her last letter, she told him that the environmentalist movement amounted to a crowd of elitists who were, in the long run, enemies of the working class. She seemed to be moving back into a political phase, and, judging from some of the people he had written about in the Behavior section, Becker figured that it was only a matter of time before she joined some kind of religious movement. Then he heard nothing.

He cut across Forty-sixth, and then walked uptown on Fifth. He was on his way to have lunch with Dick Chiles, a former writer in National News who had hit it rich with a novel based on a Palestinian guerilla plot to kidnap the society editor of the *Washington Post—A Long Way from Georgetown*. Chiles's second blockbuster was about a crazed English professor who kidnapped the nation's most famous talk-show host and refused to release him "until everybody's sentences parse." By his third book, Chiles had only to show the publisher a one sentence synopsis of the plot ("It's about a kidnapping") to get what was reputed to be a three hundred thousand dollar advance, a sixty-forty split on the paperback sale, and a permanently reserved table at Antonio's, a midtown Italian restaurant favored by the publishing set.

It was at Antonio's that Chiles suggested they meet, after Becker phoned to say he might need some advice. Antonio's was a small, dim place in the East Fifties, with a decor that a restaurant critic had described as being capable of inducing claustrophobia in a coal miner. The same critic maintained a standing offer of dinner for two at Lutece for anybody who could distinguish Antonio's spaghetti from its calamari by taste or texture ("A blindfold will not be required; it also looks the same."). Reservations were almost impossible to come by less than a month in advance.

Becker arrived a few minutes early, but was seated immediately by Antonio himself—a dark, excessively deferential man wearing a black silk shirt and four gold chains. Becker had been in Antonio's only once before—when, as the temporary writer of the Books section, he was assigned a story on a sudden publishing house shakeup that had resulted in the firing of Waldo Brookside, one of the best-known editors in New York. Charles Shopsin, the senior editor whose responsibilities included the Books section, had decided that Becker should interview Brookside personally, resulting in one of the few forays he had made into reporting aside from his tour in Washington. Becker had been uneasy about the assignment since he wasn't certain he could bring himself to ask Brookside about some of the information Shopsin wanted in the story—exactly why he was fired, for instance, and what sort of financial settlement had been made. Becker had been brought up not to pry. Even if he were able to ask such questions, Becker wondered before he met Waldo Brookside, how would he get around the evasive answers Brookside would presumably give? What would induce anybody to reveal his private thoughts about an obviously embarrassing reversal—particularly at Antonio's, where the seating arrangements seemed to guarantee every customer the benefit of every other customer's conversation?

Brookside had turned out to be a skinny little man wearing a heavy turtleneck sweater and aviator glasses with lenses that seemed to be almost the size of Antonio's butter plates. To Becker's astonishment, Brookside had sat down, given him a perfunctory handshake, nodded at the waiter as a signal to bring his customary Campari-and-soda, and said, "I was only in it for the nooky, you know."

Becker fumbled for his notebook. "I beg your pardon," he said, assuming that he might have misunderstood.

"The nooky. The poontang. The tail," Brookside said, sipping the Campari that had appeared at his elbow, and nodding at acquaintances around the restaurant—all of whom nodded back, either in greeting or in agreement with his statement. "You'd be surprised how much of that an important editor in chief runs across. Or perhaps you wouldn't be surprised. Well, at any rate. Secretaries, of course. Aspiring female novelists of the sensitive girlhood sort rather than the feminist sort. Agents. I don't go for agents much, but they're there. Yes, indeed. Agents. Then there's the hanger-on types who like to be with the literati. It was really quite splendid—all that nooky. I'll miss that part. I don't mind telling you that I never used to get many girls. I mean before."

Becker was scribbling furiously. He hadn't even had a chance to ask Brookside a question.

"In college, I was a wonk," Brookside said. "I don't even want to talk about high school." He shuddered.

"A what?" Becker asked, relieved that he had finally been able to get in a question.

"A wonk. A weenie. A wimp," Brookside said. "Even after college I was a wonk." He spoke matter-of-factly, as if outlining the plot of a new novel. "I was a wonk right up until I was made editor in chief. Then nobody thought I was a wonk anymore. I don't know if not being editor in chief means that I'm a wonk again. It's an interesting question."

Becker nodded, sorry he hadn't asked it, and flipped the page of his notebook. He was having trouble keeping up.

"Yes, the nooky's all I'll miss," Brookside went on. "I didn't really need the money, and Antonio says that I can keep my table here at least through the end of the year. I certainly won't miss having to read all those books. I don't know which I hate more—books or authors. That's another interesting question. Oh, authors, I think. Yes, authors. Definitely. Put down authors."

"Hates authors more than books," Becker wrote obediently, while Brookside tilted his head sideways to make certain Becker got it down correctly.

"Of course, they didn't like me either," Brookside said. "Silly twits. Some of them, I'm sure, thought I was still a wonk, even though I was the editor in chief. Some of them hated me just because they'd walk into bookstores and couldn't find their books. It wasn't my fault they couldn't find their precious books. Silly twits. Do you know how many books were dedicated to me during my nine years as editor in chief?"

Becker, still scribbling away as fast as he could, shook his head.

"One book," Brookside said. "One lousy book. Also, a lousy book, as it happens. *The Basil and Fennell Cookbook.* Not even a novel. A cookbook. Even at that, the only reason she dedicated it to me was that she happened to be in my group, and I talked in group a lot about how nobody had ever dedicated a book to me. She dedicated the book to me just because she was in my group. For that matter, I published the book just because she was in my group: I figured she might dedicate it to me. Goodness knows she didn't have anybody else to dedicate it to, judging from what she talked about in group. 'To Waldo, with admiration and understanding.' The part about understanding was a giveaway, of course. People who read it probably realized she had done it just because I was in her group. If anybody read it, because you couldn't find the damned thing in the bookstores."

Now, sitting at Antonio's, waiting for Dick Chiles, Becker wondered what ever happened to Waldo Brookside. Had he gone back to being a wonk? Had he fetched up at another publishing house—perhaps a publishing house that might be interested in a blockbuster novel set in the White House? The Cabinet Room again floated into Becker's mind. One after another, the cabinet secretaries and generals and presidential advisers who are gathered around the table stand up to suggest what course of action should be taken about the President's wife. The Secretary of State speaks to the question of whether or not the Russian ambassador should be called in. The Russian ambassador! Could that be? The Russian ambassador was always called in by the President in White House novels. Maybe he would have to be called in to be assured that all of the unusual activity at the White House was not of a military nature. "And why, may I ask," the Russian ambassador would say, "has General Lingeman been summoned here seven times in the past three days? Does he, perhaps, have midwifery capabilities?"

General Lingeman, a carefully turned-out West Pointer who has been fiddling with his class ring while waiting to speak, does have what he refers to as "some field experience" in awkward pregnancies—a dalliance with his secretary, perhaps, or with the Secretary of Commerce, who, during the speeches of other presidential advisers, has been sending him looks fraught (not pregnant; there were limits to this thing) with meaning. If the Secretary of Commerce is a woman, though, it might seem rather inappropriate for the Secretary of State to deliver the news to the cabinet by saying, "Gentlemen, the President's wife is pregnant." Becker loved that phrase. Perhaps General

Lingeman's liaison was with a female general, or with the first woman to command a combat paratroop regiment. But couldn't she induce a miscarriage any time she wanted to simply by jumping out of an airplane? Perhaps not. Lingeman begins his presentation by saying what a pity it is that the navy's security arrangements at Walter Reed do not happen to be up to the task at hand. The Navy Chief of Staff stirs in his chair, the temper that cost him a broken metatarsus at Leyte always in danger of exploding. Fortunately, General Lingeman says, the army has a "strategic parade-ployment system" that can put the First Lady in the hands of a certain medical corps lieutenant colonel stationed at an army hospital in Micronesia.

The Secretary of Labor, Matt Murphy, is waiting impatiently to speak his mind. He is a bit coarse—his initial locker-room reaction to the news of the First Lady's condition being but one of several examples in the opening chapters—but he is basically a decent and honest American workingman who can be counted on when the going gets rough. He is the most trustworthy of the President's inner circle. (The least trustworthy, of course, is the National Security Council director, an oily and opportunistic bureaucrat modeled down to small details on Ralph Holbrook—perhaps with a name like Ralph Smiler, on the off chance that anybody at the magazine needed further hints.) When Lingeman sits down, Matt Murphy rises from his chair, and looks directly at the President. "If you make her go to one of those back-alley butchers, it'll be on your immortal soul forever, Mr. President," he says. "And if you want to fire me for saying so, so be it."

Breaking the silence that follows, Ralph Smiler says, "I'm sure the Secretary of Labor didn't mean—"

"I meant exactly what I said, you smarmy little pissant," Murphy says, glowering at Smiler, who smiles weakly and says nothing. Murphy begins throwing papers into his briefcase, ready to leave the room, but the President, knowing the value of a straight-talker and a loyal friend, motions him back to his seat. The Secretary of State nods at Murphy and smiles in understanding and support and even affection. They are, despite the disparity of their backgrounds, fast friends—united by mutual respect and a shared contempt for Ralph Smiler.

"Perhaps you'd like to give us the benefit of your thinking on this matter, Ralph," the President says to Smiler.

For the first time since the secretary of state opened the meeting, there are smiles around the conference table. Everyone knows that Smiler's "field experience," trying to lure secretaries into the White House fallout shelter, has amounted to a series of dreadfully embarrassing failures. When he finally managed to spend the night there with a bookkeeper of surpassing ugliness, he contracted a social disease even though he proved to be impotent. Becker was smiling as Dick Chiles sat down.

Chiles was a tall, rather awkward man with arms that seemed slightly too long for him. In Becker's memory of him, Chiles always appeared dressed the way most writers at the magazine dressed—slightly frayed sport jacket, tie slightly askew. By the time of the publication party for his second book, though, Chiles was in an open-necked sport shirt and no jacket. Now, he was dressed pretty much the way Antonio was—a black shirt unbuttoned halfway down his chest. Another paperback sale or two, Becker figured, and Chiles wouldn't be wearing any shirt at all.

Except for his clothing, though, Chiles had not been greatly affected by the comforting squeeze he had received from the golden claw. He made an occasional reference to "upfront money" or "points," but he seemed to prefer talking about which couple Andy Wolferman had seen where or which unsuspecting soul might be doomed to become bureau chief in Ottawa. He still dropped by the Bamboo Gardens now and then and joined in the general griping about Syracuse Smiley as if he remained vulnerable to Smiley's machinations.

"How are things at the word factory?" he said.

"About the same," Becker said. "There's been a lot of talk about Woody leaving and Syracuse Smiley getting his job. They've never had a managing editor who was never a reporter, but that's getting to be our only hope. Andy figures Holbrook's going to try to pull off some reporting coup to make Towndsend forget about that—maybe find out that pigeons are an endangered species or something."

"You're smart to look for a way out, then," Chiles said, as he glanced over the menu. "I think Smiley would turn that place into the Gulag." It was Chiles who had given Holbrook the name Syracuse Smiley. Until then, the writers had been making do with N.R.F. (for No Redeeming Features) or simply the Shithead. Chiles was also the writer—Becker and one other person knew—who returned to the magazine late one Friday night, slipped into the make-up room, and changed a story Holbrook had personally edited so that it appeared in the magazine saying that unrestricted poaching on the East African wildebeest herd might be an efficient way to increase the protein intake of local tribesmen. To the disappointment of those who figured that Chiles's caper might have slowed Holbrook's progress toward the managing editorship, there was no reaction from Towndsend, who had been incommunicado in Mauritius, observing large lizards. Holbrook's attempts to find the culprit had at least provided some entertainment; signs still popped up now and then, in the hallway or the men's room or the interoffice mail, saying Beware of the Phantom Diddler.

"Don't tell me the plot," Chiles said, after they had ordered. Becker had said over the telephone only that his idea was for a novel set in Washington. "I wouldn't steal it, but around here the waiter might. Everyone's in the business here. I wouldn't be surprised to hear that the dishwasher has a thriller set in Ponce hidden in the pots-and-pans cupboard. I used to wonder why everybody in publishing goes to a restaurant where you can't say anything without half the other publishers and writers and agents in town hearing what you're saying. Then I realized that they come here because they want to hear what everybody else is saying. Then—this is the real breakthrough—I finally realized that they also come here because they want everyone else to hear what *they're* saying. It's the way they get the word around. One guy tells another guy at lunch that the entire future of his company is riding on Joe Shmuck's novel *Up the Queen's,* and the editor at the next table starts talking to some agent he's having lunch with about *Up the Queen's,* and the agent talks to one of his clients who happens to be a reviewer, and pretty soon what turns up on the front page of the book review sections and has fifty thousand copies in print and gets big bucks for paperback and they're bidding on the movie rights but *Up the Queen's.* Antonio ought to get ten percent. It's not just that he provides a place with tables jammed so close together that you're always in danger of putting a forkful of spaghetti into someone else's mouth. He serves food that is so bad that eating is held to a minimum—so a customer very rarely misses anything important because of not being able to hear well while he's chewing his veal Marsala. Everybody knows it's impossible to chew the veal Marsala Antonio serves, so nobody tries."

A man at the next table nodded, and rolled his eyes toward the ceiling to indicate his experience with Antonio's veal Marsala.

"I'd be happy to tell you the plot—at least as much as I've figured out," Becker said. He thought he noticed a couple of people at nearby tables react by leaning a bit closer, but it might have been his imagination.

"Please, no," Chiles said, holding up his hand. "I don't know much about plots anyway. I just move the one I know from field to field and country to country, and write off the travel expenses. My only serious expertise is in matters like advances and paperback deals. If you're using my plot, I'd appreciate acknowledgement in the form of having a minor but charming character named after me; otherwise, let's talk about money. And please speak up."

"Well, I should tell you at least that it's set in the White House," Becker said, still speaking in a rather quiet voice.

"Auction it with a floor of a hundred thousand," Chiles said. "Only way to go." Everyone seemed to be looking over at their table. Suddenly, Becker couldn't hear another word being spoken in the restaurant. Some people seemed to have been frozen with forks halfway to their mouths—as if in a stop-frame in a film.

"Floor bid of a hundred thousand?" Becker asked, raising his voice a bit.

"Look, Fred, this one's obviously going to be a blockbuster," Chiles said. "We're not talking about lyrical memories of adolescence in Cornwall here. This is big bucks. Big bucks. Also, I think you're crazy if you don't demand a seventy-thirty split on the paperback. And you know already what I think about the key to the movie deal."

"Points?" Becker said.

"Right. Sure. Points. Of course points," Chiles replied. "But points on the gross, not on the net. You give those bastards out there a chance, they'll write off their new sound system and eight bar mitzvahs and the invasion of Normandy against the profits, and the movie'll gross twenty million and you'll never see a pea." Several people at other tables nodded in agreement.

"The man speaks the truth," the waiter said, as he brought some bread and butter. "Never talk net. Always talk gross." The listeners nodded again.

After lunch, as he walked down Fifth Avenue with Chiles, Becker said, "I could tell you a little about the characters, if you think that would help give you an idea of what it might be like."

"Don't worry about the characters; concentrate on the title," Chiles said. "The title's the thing. I would consider it a personal favor, of course, if you could see your way clear to having one character who is modeled on Syracuse Smiley and gets the clap."

"How did you know?"

"You're kidding!" Chiles said. "You really have a character like that? So do I—in the new one. That's great. Maybe we can encourage everyone who writes a novel to do it, and then have some doctoral candidate trace it for his thesis, 'Clapped Out: The Depiction of Ralph Holbrook in Contemporary American Trash Novels.' "

"It'd make a good piece for the Books section."

"I really think this may be the golden claw for you, Fred," Chiles said. "The Antonio's crowd seemed very interested. I think I saw Herb Winer drop a spoonful of minestrone in his lap when we talked about what the German rights might be worth. The White House is very big these days. It's just too bad you weren't mixed up in Watergate in some way."

"I was thinking the same thing," Becker said. "I don't even have a misdemeanor against me."

"Jesus, those guys cashed in," Chiles said. "If I had known the kind of bucks they were talking about, I would have confessed to the whole damned thing. The break-in, the cover-up, paying the hoods, taping the door, taping the tapes, erasing the tapes, you name it."

"Well, it's too late for that now, I guess," Becker said.

They stopped on a corner in the Forties, where Chiles had to turn off to see his accountant. Becker thanked him, and promised to call if he decided to go ahead with the novel—Chiles having offered to help find an agent and someone he called a freelance packaging consultant.

"Oh, by the way," Becker said. "Being at Antonio's reminded me: do you know whatever happened to Waldo Brookside? Is he all right?"

"All right!" Chiles said. "I would say he's all right. He wrote one of those reveal-all books about getting fired. A hundred big ones up front. Full selection book club. The guys on the coast are fighting among themselves to see

which one gets to screw up the movie. Half a mil paperback."

"What's the name of it?"

"It's called *No More Nooky*," Chiles said. "He got the
hundred thou just on the title."

14 Near the bank of elevators in the lobby, Becker saw Pam Robinson. She gave him the thumbs-up sign. "Doc's in pretty good shape," she said. "I think that preventive medicine piece from last week overtook the narcolepsy piece somewhere in his blood stream and had enough left over to knock out the bilharzia symptoms. I think he might last the week."

When the elevator door opened at his floor, Becker walked out—and right into Ralph Holbrook, whose gaze was fixed not on the elevator but on the end of a pipe he was trying to light.

"Oh, sorry, Ralph," Becker said.

"Just the man I wanted to see," Holbrook said. "I'll walk you to your office." He flashed what the writers called his hangman's smile and started down the hall with Becker. "How've you been, Fred? How's the family?"

"I'm divorced," Becker said.

"Yes, of course. Sorry. I forgot," Holbrook said. "Sometimes it's the best course of action for everyone concerned. Even the children."

"We didn't have any children," Becker said, but Holbrook was already on a different subject.

"You know Pat Powers is going to Rio for us, Fred," he said. "And that leaves an opening in Foreign Affairs. It might be a good bet for you—a good card to have in your pack a little later on. Nothing you have to do if you don't want to, of course. We're not going to force anybody to write anywhere he doesn't want to write, of course, if we can help it. You know that. Nothing you have to decide right away, either; Pat won't be leaving for another three weeks, and even then you could try Foreign Affairs as a floater for a few weeks before we made it permanent. I think you should think about it pretty hard, though, Fred. We can talk more next week."

They had reached the Lifestyle writer's office. "Sure. O.K.," Becker said. "We'll talk about it. Thanks."

"Great, Fred," Holbrook said, leaving him with a light pat on the shoulder. "Regards to the family."

It was known that "think about it pretty hard" was Smiley's way of saying "do it." Becker knew that refusing to subject himself to an eternal Cyprus dispute in the Foreign Affairs section would not mean getting fired. He was a quick, clear writer—stable enough to switch back and forth between Medicine and Religion without becoming seriously queasy or having a spiritual crisis. He was too useful to be fired. If Syracuse Smiley wanted to pressure him, though, it might be a long time between raises. Even worse, Becker might be fed long doses of Business or Religion as a way of enhancing his appreciation of Foreign Affairs. Was Cyprus really worse than that horde of clerical press agents?

He could appeal such a harsh sentence to Woody Fenton, of course. It might be possible to go over Smiley's head once more. What would happen, though, if there came a time when there was nobody over Smiley's head? Would Becker find his job unbearable? For the first time since he was in the Washington bureau, Becker gave serious consideration to what life would be like if he left the magazine. Sometimes, he thought he would greatly miss the magazine's daily goings on—the report of Pete Smithers' latest explosion, the jokes about Milt Silvers' move from a converted boxcar to a former cheese factory. Sometimes, Becker found the familiarity of such stories comforting—like old stories families tell about eccentric cousins and black sheep uncles and lost fortunes. Sometimes, though, the magazine began to feel like some Caribbean harbor where everyone had known everyone else too long and for too many hours a day and for too many heart-to-hearts late at night after too many rums. If he did move on, of course, it would be more comfortable moving with the cushion of what Dick Chiles called "big bucks."

Becker hung up his jacket and sat down behind the desk. His in-box was almost full. There were copies of a number of queries Carol Goodenow had sent to the bureaus—and the first response they had received to their roundup query on two-thirds stockings. It was from the Atlanta bureau. It said, "No two-thirds stockings here. O'Hearn." Becker was not surprised. Frank O'Hearn was known for his impatience with roundup queries. Becker still remembered his answer to the yo-yo query: "Re your yo-yo query, we're framing that one." Becker knew—and he assumed Carol Goodenow knew—that there would be plenty of two-thirds stockings in Chicago or Boston or Houston.

The in-box also contained a memo from Woody Fenton. An article from the *Baltimore Sun* about someone in Maryland who produced goose liver by force-feeding geese in the French manner had been pinned to a piece of copy paper with an ordinary straight pin. Next to it was the single word "Wow!" written in red pencil. As usual, Becker had no idea how to interpret the message. Was Fenton merely saying that force-feeding geese was a remarkable phenomenon? Did he want a piece done on the goose liver that resulted? Could it be that the geese in question were not considered domestic fowl but wild game in captivity and were therefore eligible for Edward Towndsend's special concern? Becker shrugged and got out his expandable cardboard file in order to add the goose liver comment to his collection of golly memos.

He found himself thumbing through some of the old memos—he loved the one that consisted of an item on a devastating earthquake in Pakistan and a scrawled "gosh!"—and then through the three or four letters from Greta he had kept. One of them had been sent in an envelope that must have originally held a telephone bill. It had the characteristic address window and a trace of what might have been a New England Bell logo visible on the back flap under the markings of three other return addresses, which had been written in and then blacked out as the envelope was used again and again. The letter inside, as far as Becker could tell, had been written on what was originally a flyer from a mung bean co-op. Greta's writing was not easy to make out, since it followed a rather haphazard path around the mung bean announcements and what appeared to be two or three previous letters written by papersavers. "Dear Fred," it began, "Wednesday, I went into town with the community's shopping unit, thinking my alimony check would be at the post office. It was not. That meant that I had to return yesterday, using more than .43 gal. of IFF." In a couple of previous letters based on the proposition that being late with alimony payments was a way of destroying the environment, Becker had learned that IFF meant Irreplaceable Fossil Fuels. "I know such matters are of little importance to you," the letter went on. "You with your plastic-wrapped suits from the cleaners and your petroleum by-product plastic wrapping around your nonreturnable tonic bottle and your hypocritical friends who claim to be celebrating life while using disposable diapers. But how can you foist your anti-earth views on me?"

Becker knew that he was stalling, trying to put off the moment of calling Mary Jane Wheeler at the White House. Was he really up to calling Mary Jane Wheeler and asking her what was or wasn't going on in the First Lady's ovaries? Why would she tell him? Why would she have told Leonard Wentzell, for that matter? Wentzell, after all, was the one who had thrown a root beer float down her dress. Of course, that was a long time ago—when the three of them were juniors in high school—but it was not the sort of thing someone forgets easily. Wentzell, certainly, had never been allowed to forget what came out of their altercation—the despised nickname Rug Merchant.

It was at a sort of club or community hall on Lake Pomme de Terre—one of those small, brown Nebraska lakes that the Corps of Engineers seemed to scoop out of the prairie here and there on its way to a more significant hydro-electric project. Mary Jane Wheeler, in a low-cut white dress that she had obviously bought specifically for the dance, was walking by a group of three or four boys when Wentzell said—in a louder voice than he realized, as it turned out—"Will you get a look at that pair of Howards!" It happened to be a period in their lives when, as Becker later recalled, Wentzell knew fifty-eight words for the female breast.

There was a moment of horrified silence, as Mary Jane, her face red, her hands trembling, stared at Leonard Wentzell. "A look is all you'd ever get," Mary Jane finally said. "You—you *rug merchant!*"

For the first time anyone could remember, Leonard Wentzell was without a reply. The reason for his having been struck mute was obvious to everyone: Mary Jane Wheeler, in her fury, had somehow stumbled onto one of those childhood nicknames that would be impossible to shake. There had been attempts before to give Wentzell some sort of name that would account for his Levantine appearance—Turk, camel-jockey, Sultan—but none of them had stuck. Nobody in the school knew precisely what nationality the term "rug merchant" denoted. From the moment the phrase was out of Mary Jane Wheeler's mouth, though, everybody somehow knew that years from then Leonard Wentzell would be unable to meet anyone from home without being asked for the price of an eight-by-ten Persian or being told that he seemed to be holding up pretty well for someone who was on his hands and knees tacking down carpets all day. Wentzell, of course, knew it best of all. So, in a moment of violence quite uncharacteristic of his childhood, he threw the root beer float he happened to be holding down the front of Mary Jane Wheeler's brand-new white dress.

How, after all these years, was Becker supposed to go about asking Mary Jane Wheeler about the First Lady's condition? He had imagined what the conversation might be like: "Mary Jane? It's Fred. What? Fred Becker. From home. Right, Freddy Becker. The same. The one with what? Oh, yes. I'm not sure I'd hoped to be remembered as the one with the kind of mangy-looking dog, but I suppose that's one way to describe me. . . . Yes, it has been a long time. Eighteen years? It's been that long? Well. Yes. A long time. I just wanted to call and say that all of us are certainly proud to see the success you've had, Mary Jane, right there in the thick of the ethnic thing and all. I was talking to Leonard Wentzell about it, and he just happened to mention that you might—well, seeing that you're right there and all. Well. Mary Jane, is she preggers or isn't she?"

Suddenly, almost without thinking, Becker picked up the telephone, dialed the White House, and asked for Mary Jane Wheeler.

"Office of the special assistant for interethnicity," a crisp female voice said.

"Is Mary Jane Wheeler in, please?"

There was a long silence. "Just one moment, please," the secretary said. Becker heard himself being put on hold—a familiar sound from his days of phoning State Department desk men—and then, after a couple of minutes, the secretary's voice came back on the phone.

"May I ask who's calling, please?" she said.

"This is Fred Becker, an old friend of Miss Wheeler's,"

Becker said. It occurred to him that he should have mentioned the magazine. The secretary might have been given instructions to put off all old friends from Nebraska who were in Washington for the Shrine convention or something and expected Mary Jane to spend an afternoon showing them through the White House and the Washington Monument. Before he could add anything, though, he was on hold again.

"I'm afraid she cannot be reached," the secretary said, when she again came on the line.

"You mean she's out for the day?"

"Not just the day."

"She does still work there, doesn't she?"

"Could you hold the line just a moment, please?" the secretary said. He was on hold again for a minute or two. Then the secretary came back on. "Yes," she said.

There was a long silence. Finally, Becker said, "Well, I'd really like to talk to her. Is there anyplace else I could reach her?"

"Hold the line for a moment, please," the secretary said. Again he found himself on hold. Then the secretary came back on the line and said, "No."

"Could you tell me what her status is?" Becker said. "Maybe without going off the line."

"Just a moment, please," the secretary said, going off the line. After another two or three minutes, she returned to say, "Ms. Wheeler is specially detached."

"Detached?"

"Specially detached."

"Could you tell me what that means?"

"No."

Finally, Becker thanked the secretary and hung up. He leaned back in his desk chair and tried to figure out the conversation. Why had the Rug Merchant told him to call Mary Jane Wheeler if Mary Jane Wheeler was specially detached? What could specially detached possibly mean? After a few minutes, Becker tried to go over the queries Carol Goodenow had sent to the bureaus, but he couldn't get Mary Jane Wheeler out of his mind.

He was startled by the jangle of the telephone.

"Pal of my youth," Leonard Wentzell said. "Have you called her yet?"

Becker told Wentzell about the conversation with the secretary in the Office of the Special Assistant for Interethnicity.

"Oh, my God!" Wentzell said. "I hope she's all right!"

"All right! Why shouldn't she be all right?"

"These people play for keeps, Federico, and they've got a lot riding on this one."

"You mean you think someone might have wanted to do her harm?"

"Talk to you later, Freddy, my man. I've got to call some people."

Feeling the need for a walk or a drink, Becker pulled his jacket back on and walked to the elevator bank. He stepped into the corner elevator, which, as usual, had movers' pads hung around the walls. The corner elevator was presumably used to move office furniture from one floor to another, but Becker had never got over the feeling that a padded elevator was necessary for transporting the rhymes-with man to and from a cage hidden in some secret corner of the twentieth floor. Although the magazine customarily dealt with a difficult to pronounce word by explaining inside parentheses what it rhymed with, no writer Becker knew had ever written one of the parenthetical explanations. Becker had always accounted for their presence in the magazine by assuming them to be the product of a single rhymes-with man—a half-mad poet who paced his hidden cage, cackling and throwing off couplets. A padded elevator was just the thing for taking the rhymes-with man out for exercise—late at night, with his keeper. When riding the corner elevator, Becker always imagined the rhymes-with man dashing from wall to wall of the car on his chain, knocking his head against the padding now and then to jar out a rhyme, and chanting whatever rhymes he had produced that day: Ratatouille rhymes with lotta hooey. Pago Pago rhymes with bongo bongo. Lateiner rhymes with a shiner. De Vries rhymes with the trees, if you please. Also a sneeze. Talese does not rhyme with a sneeze. Almost. Nan Talese rhymes with ban the geese. Nukualofa rhymes with move the sofa. Tisha B'ov rhymes with fish in love. Nevis rhymes with leave us. Fiji rhymes with P.G. P.G. Wodehouse rhymes with Fiji wood mouse. Mary Jane Wheeler. Mary Wheeler rhymes with bury squealer.

15 "Does he know we've sent queries on two-thirds stockings?" Becker whispered to Genine McIntyre at the door to Pete Smithers' office.

"Not yet," she whispered. "Better not bring it up."

Woody Fenton having decided that the story on the sex change capital of the world should be in Medicine rather than Lifestyle, Smithers had called an update story conference so that the Lifestyle section could bolster its depleted story list. Becker and Carol Goodenow and Keith Johnson and Genine McIntyre and a brace of photo researchers were again filing into the senior editor's office.

"All right, Fred," the voice from behind and below Smithers' desk said, once everyone was settled. "Whadawe got now?"

"Nothing really great, I'm afraid," Becker said, flipping over a couple of the sheets on his clipboard. "I don't know how you feel about this one from Chicago about people wrapping these big Lake Michigan fish in aluminum foil and then steaming them in their automatic dishwashers."

"Jesus!" Smithers said.

Becker sometimes found one of Smithers' Jesuses as

difficult to interpret as a golly from Woody Fenton. "No detergent," he added, without quite knowing why. "Two cycles."

"Didn't we do fish in dishwashers?" Smithers said. "Genine?"

"We did bacon with steam irons," Genine said. "And Medicine last year did interns grilling baby shrimp with cauteries."

"Is it like a trend?" Smithers asked.

"I don't think any of them are connected, Pete," Becker said. "I mean, it's not like there's a fad so that some people are frying eggs on Pontiac radiators and other people are whipping cream with chain saws."

There was a long silence. "Jesus," Smithers finally said. There was another long silence. Then Smithers said, "What's next?" The voice remained below the desk. Becker still hadn't seen anything of Smithers except the bottom of his shoes.

Becker flipped a couple more pages on his clipboard. There was a suggestion from the Chicago bureau about people collecting antique sink stoppers—antique, in this case, roughly corresponding to the years of the war in Korea. "Sink stoppers?" Becker said, rather tentatively.

The only noise that came from behind Smithers' desk was some mumbling. It was difficult to make out, but Becker thought he might have heard, "Holy Jesus. Mother of God."

"That last piece on the collectors' convention in Atlantic City was on ice-cream scoops, not sink stoppers," Genine McIntyre said, apparently anticipating Smithers' question.

"What else you got, Fred?" Smithers said. His voice sounded weary.

"Well, we could revive this suggestion on Angus Mc-Taggart, the microgardener." McTaggart was the inventor of a theory of gardening based roughly on the principle that constant mulching of the soil with a combination of sea-weed and insect leavings and a certain sort of pipe tobacco could produce steadily increasing yields on steadily dimin-ishing garden plots—so that, according to his teachings, the vegetable requirements of a family of four could eventu-ally be fulfilled by a garden plot the size of an ordinary throw rug.

"Is he the guy who dropped out of Wall Street?" Smithers asked.

"Right. That's the guy," Becker said. He was en-couraged. At least Smithers had asked a civil question. "He was one of those guys who specialized in finding corpora-tions that could be counted on to lose a lot of money for guys who needed tax losses. They say he bought this agribusiness conglomerate that looked good for some pretty disastrous losses, but then it looked like the damned thing was going to make a profit, so he went out to Michigan to find out what was going wrong, and it turned out it was all because of this one little applesauce canning plant near Benton Har-bor."

"Yeah, yeah. Now I'm starting to remember," Smithers said. "And there was some sort of squarehead con-nected to it somehow."

"Well, this old Swede did run the plant, and sup-posedly, through this special orcharding method, he had reduced the acreage they were planting so that they had only eighteen apple trees giving all these apples—although the other version of the story is that the old Swede was able to make all this profit because he broke an apple-pickers strike by importing a lot of Mexican illegals from Chicago. Anyway, the Swede became McTaggart's guru, and McTaggart extended the method of orcharding to vegetable gardening, and quit Wall Street, and became a big guru himself. Now he claims that he could feed India with a garden the size of the main waiting room at Grand Central."

"Where did I just read about this, though?" Smithers said. "I didn't read more than a sentence or two of that old suggestion, but this sounds familiar."

"I don't know where you could have read it, Pete."

"Anybody else? Does that sound familiar to anybody else?" The room was silent. "Genine? You got any ideas?"

"It was in the magazine this week," Genine McIntyre said. "The Business section did an eighty-liner on McTaggart this week."

Nobody said anything for a while. "Oh," Becker finally said. He looked at Carol Goodenow and shrugged.

Pete Smithers took his feet off his desk. Very slowly, he straightened up in his chair until he was sitting upright behind his desk. The room was still silent. "Let me get this straight," Smithers said, in a voice Becker considered ominously controlled. "This story on McTaggart was in our very own magazine this week, and nobody here knew that except Genine?"

A couple of the other people in the room shrugged and nodded. Becker had never read a Business story he hadn't written, and he assumed that the Business section reading of the others was similarly circumscribed.

"Jesus Christ!" Smithers shouted. "Jesus H. Christ!" The photo researchers, looking alarmed, instinctively moved closer to each other. "I could have gone into Woody with a new story list that included not just a story about some stupid sons of bitches washing sturgeon and a story about some other stupid sons of bitches collecting sink stoppers but a story that already ran in this very magazine—this very week! Jesus Christ! Fred, goddamn it, are you trying to tell me that's all you have to offer—a story that has already been in the goddamned magazine?"

Becker thumbed through the papers on his clipboard again. He didn't blame Smithers for being upset about the McTaggart story, but Smithers knew as well as anyone that the section's writer—particularly a writer who was a floater doing Lifestyle for only a week—could not be held responsible for coming up with a new story list on short notice Tuesday afternoon. Becker had no private supply of Lifestyle suggestions—except for Yitzchak Katz's kosher fast-food chain, which was hardly a story if it had not even got to the point of deciding on a name. Wentzell's suggestion about Akron crossed Becker's mind, but he dismissed it. He leafed through the papers on his clipboard again. He couldn't seem to find anything.

"Well," Smithers said. "Are we all just going to sit here, Fred?"

"Well," Becker finally said. "There is one other possibility. We haven't had a suggestion on it, but I happen to know about it from another source. It's in Akron. It appears that vice squad cops there, when they have some time on their hands, make a sweep of men's rooms in movie theaters and bus stations and all to see if—" He looked over at Carol Goodenow, who was concentrating very hard on her clipboard. "—Well, to see if people are in there, uh, performing, well, what the vice squad calls, sort of, acts of oral sex, if you know what I mean."

Carol was definitely blushing. Smithers seemed to be muttering something like "goddamned pansies," but since he had returned to his customary position below the desk it was difficult to tell. Becker had begun to wish that Wentzell had never told him about the Akron story. Now that he had begun, though, there seemed no choice but to continue.

"So," he went on. "What they would do is just kick open the door of the men's room and take a quick glance under the stalls to see if they could see two pair of legs anywhere instead of just one."

"That's about all we have in this magazine anymore," Smithers said, quite clearly, from behind the desk.

"Well, a lot of times, what they would see was one pair of legs and a shopping bag on the floor in front of the guy. Which seemed natural enough—a guy sitting on the—well, using the bathroom there, and he takes his shopping bag with him so nobody will steal it. And all." He glanced over at Carol. From the look on her face, he guessed that she might be using some variety of the concentration methods taught by the mystical Thai plastics tycoon. For a moment, he considered making a sudden switch to the Disneyland jungle cruise story, but that one obviously couldn't take place in Akron. He plunged on. "Then, finally, one of the cops happened to open a stall door, and he found that, in fact, there's another guy standing in the shopping bag."

Becker paused. He didn't know whether to continue. He didn't know what the continuation would be. He didn't know what had ever made him think that this bit of esoterica from Wentzell was a newsmagazine story. Smithers said nothing. Nobody else spoke.

Then Keith Johnson said, "Is that a trend?"

There was still no sound from behind the desk.

"Well, Pete," Becker said. "I guess at the very most it's a fifty-liner. If that. A little offbeat, I'll admit."

Becker paused, and again there was silence. "Pete?" Becker went on. "Are you back there, Pete?"

"I can still see his Bass Weejuns," Johnson said.

"Are there any feet in them?" Becker asked.

Johnson and Becker both stood up and walked over to Smithers' desk, where they could look down the wrong end of the gunsight. From the color of Smithers' face and the movements he was making with his mouth, it was apparent that he had been trying to speak for some time. No sound emerged.

The Countess and the photo researchers and Carol Goodenow gathered around the desk next to Becker and Johnson. "Maybe even just a thirty-liner, Pete," Becker said.

"I think I remember now reading the McTaggart piece in this week's issue, Pete," Carol Goodenow said.

"Oh, me too," Becker said.

"Fine little piece," Johnson said.

"Maybe we should continue the story conference a little later," Genine said.

The rest of them filed out of Smithers' office. Behind them, they heard the appalling drone of the senior editor's intercom. "He's just stepped away from his desk for a moment, Mr. Fenton," Genine said. "Yes. He came up with a hundred-liner that looks good—two-thirds stockings."

16 Becker cocked his head to the right to keep the telephone receiver next to his ear while he looked through his in-box to see if any files from correspondents had come in while he was at the story conference. Leonard Wentzell's telephone had already rung a dozen times, but Becker remained on the line. The first few papers he went through were memos rather than files from correspondents. There was a memo from the personnel office saying that a number of employees seemed to be filing insurance claims that disguised tooth-capping work, which was not covered, as root canals, and that the insurance company was threatening an investigation. There was a memo from Ralph Holbrook saying that the next person caught putting up a Beware of the Phantom Diddler sign would be dismissed. There was a memo from the shop steward for the guild saying that posting Beware of the Phantom Diddler signs fell within the employee free-speech section of all NLRB contracts and was also a constitutionally protected activity. Becker was not troubled by the absence of any files from correspondents. When he became restless at the beginning of a week, he sometimes started writing before the files came in. If he was having a slow Tuesday in the Entertainment Arts section when the week's list included a story on, say, neominimalist film makers, he would simply try to imagine, judging from the bureau suggestion or a newspaper clipping, what a story on neominimalist film makers might be about ("Neominimalist Ari Plotkin's latest film, shot entirely within the human nose, consists of nothing but absolute darkness and the sound of heavy breathing."). He usually found that the arrival of the files on Wednesday or Thursday called for only minor changes in the story—perhaps the insertion of a quote at the end of the first paragraph ("Says Plotkin: 'Less is already too much.' ") or the addition of some statistics. The telephone at Leonard Wentzell's continued to ring. Becker hadn't heard from the Rug Merchant since reporting the absence of Mary Jane Wheeler. Where could Wentzell be? Where could Mary Jane be?

There was no need to think that harm had befallen her. Even if Wentzell was right, and Mary Jane did know about the First Lady's pregnancy, the odd secrecy at the White House regarding her whereabouts might indicate simply that she was off doing abortion advance-work with some prominent obstetrician whose deep party connections guaranteed his silence. In Becker's novel, as it happened, the Mary Jane Wheeler character was developing into someone whose primary loyalty does not turn out to be to the First Lady and the President. She is an agent-in-place for the antiabortion loonies. Her plan is to leak the story of the First Lady's pregnancy so that the President and the First Lady have no choice but to allow it to continue. There are elements in the White House trying to stop her. By force?

Naturally by force. The manipulator of the elements is National Security Director Ralph Smiler, who would, needless to say, stop at nothing.

Becker had found that a number of characters were beginning to take shape, even though he still had no idea whether the story about the First Lady would turn out to be fact or fiction. The novel had invaded his subway thoughts. Early in the workweek, ordinarily, his thoughts on the subway tended to find their way to potential first sentences in stories he didn't really have to write until two or three days later ("Filmgoers who knew that neominimalist Ari Plotkin's newest film, *Left Nostril,* has no action at all were puzzled by Plotkin's insistence that no one be seated after the first ten minutes."). Late in the week, the rhythmic clacking of the subway train often seemed to loosen sentences that he couldn't untangle at the office ("Although the only action neominimalist Clyde Whydah includes in *Arthur's Tum* is avant-garde entrepreneur Arthur Morton scratching his stomach after the first hour, Plotkin has dismissed it as 'hopelessly cluttered.' "). Since Becker had considered the possibility of writing *The President's Wife Is Pregnant,* though, a White House staff rode the uptown IRT with him.

"The Flemish separatists are the key, of course," the White House counsel, a swarthy, unkempt man named Lawrence Weston is telling a presidential speech writer named Rod Baxter.

"Flemish separatists?" Baxter says.

Weston nods his head—a knowing nod. He is a man of some mystery. The President's enemies sometimes float the rumor that Lawrence Weston has ties to the CIA or the mob, or perhaps both. He encourages such speculation. When a newspaper columnist hinted that one of the "special projects" he took on for the President was delivering payoffs to some powerful labor leaders, Weston began showing up at White House meetings carrying a black bag instead of a briefcase.

"Why Flemish separatists?" Baxter asks.

Weston glances from side to side conspiratorially, although they are standing in the middle of the White House Rose Garden, safe from eavesdroppers or electronic bugs. "The way I see it," he says, "she visits Belgium. Some people we know provoke the Flemish separatists into a violent anti-American demonstration directed at her motorcade. She is admitted to the hospital for 'rest and observation.' The hospital happens to have on its staff a prominent gynecologist whose discretion can be assured by a certain diamond merchant who knows some World War II history the gynecologist's wife would not want to have revealed. We know some World War II history the diamond merchant would not want to have revealed."

"Maybe a little elaborate," Baxter says. By coincidence, he and Lawrence Weston are childhood acquaintances. Baxter is the generalist on the President's speechwriting staff—foreign policy one day, the energy problem the next, minority rights the day after that. Everything but religion. The President considers him invaluable. On overseas trips, Baxter always travels on Air Force One, since his presence gives the President confidence that a speech on any subject can be put together in midair at the last minute. Baxter sees a lot of the world, and gets a lot of tax-free liquor, but he always comes back to his charming rent-controlled apartment in Georgetown. Does Washington have rent control? Why not? This is fiction. If the President and the First Lady decide to have the child, it will be Rod Baxter the President turns to for a simple but eloquent announcement to end rumors of an abortion ("My wife and I ask no special credit for following the dictates of our beliefs. . . .").

Becker, at last, put down the telephone. He tried to think back to what Mary Jane Wheeler was like in high school, trying to remember whether she was from a Roman Catholic family that might have opposed abortion. All he could conjure up was the vision of her Howards.

"This, Frederic, you will certainly not believe," Wolferman said from the door.

"Probably not," Becker said.

"Romance finds a way," Wolferman said. "Couples couple. Unlikely couples couple in unlikely places."

Becker nodded, awaiting another chapter in the proving of Wolferman's Law. Suddenly, an idea for the novel flashed into his mind: maybe the reason the Mary Jane Wheeler character wants to leak the news of the First Lady's pregnancy is not that she is an agent of the antiabortion lobby. Maybe she is having just the sort of secret romance with the President that, according to Wolferman's Law, sixteen to nineteen couples at the magazine are having at any given time. Maybe Mary Jane Wheeler wants the First Lady to remain pregnant and then be saddled with an infant, so that Mary Jane and the President can be free to go on meeting at Joe Horn Dimey's Bar or whatever the presidential equivalent is. Mary Jane Wheeler in the novel or Mary Jane Wheeler? Mary Jane Wheeler in the novel, of course.

She is leaking the news now to a straight-shooting young journalist from her hometown. Like Rod Baxter but with a different name. Brad Dexter. Knowing her from the old days, Dexter can tell that her motive is not really anti-abortion zeal—partly because of the way she talks about the President.

"Brad," she says, as her fingers nervously move around the potato chips left in the bowl on the table of the dark Washington bar they chose as a meeting place. "Brad, the President is a good man."

"I know, I know," Brad says, touching her hand lightly in support.

"I mean, Brad, he's no pig fart."

"Of course he's not," Brad says. "We all know that, really."

"Now Ralph Smiler," she says. "There's a pig fart for you."

"Are you listening, Fred?" Wolferman said. "You know very well that not having an attentive audience depresses me."

"Oh, yeah. Sorry. Go ahead."

"Well, today I stuck my head in to see if you wanted to have some lunch, and you were gone."

"I had lunch with Dick Chiles."

"Right. Anyway, I started walking over to the Bamboo Gardens when who looms in front of me on Forty-sixth Street but Milt Silvers. I'm standing there. An open target. He opens his mouth—undoubtedly to tell me, in excruciating detail, about having just returned from putting down some earnest money on an abandoned grain elevator he plans to use as a summer house, and how impetuous it all was. Then, quick as a flash, I pat my back pocket and say, 'Christ! My wallet! It's on my desk!' And I turn and run. I have to say that I'm pretty quick at thinking on my feet, Frederic. I would make a very good pro quarterback, except for clumsiness and cowardice. But I know Milt is still there, blocking my way to the Gardens, ready to tell me about the great new houseplant he just got that eats goats. I was thinking about going around the block and sneaking up on the Gardens from the rear. But then I thought, what the hell, I'd go down to Hymie's on the Lower East Side and have a little of that mushroom-and-barley soup I love."

"Wait a minute," Becker said. "Stop right there. You were going all the way from midtown to a kosher dairy restaurant on the Lower East Side, all by yourself, for lunch?"

"Correct."

"When there are four dairy restaurants within walking distance of this office—including one that won the matzoh brei prize three years in a row?"

"Matzoh brei, but not mushroom-and-barley soup," Wolferman said. "I like Hymie's mushroom-and-barley soup. Also, I like the atmosphere. The waiter is one of those Lower East Side Jewish waiters who's heard too many Jewish waiter stories, so he thinks he's obliged to be rude. You order mushroom-and-barley soup, he brings you matzoh ball soup. If you complain, he tells you it's none of your business. Sometimes, he says, 'Don't make such a deal from it. If you want to make such a deal from it, go to some joint with the Irishers.' "

"I thought you liked the mushroom-and-barley soup."

"I do. That's why I order the matzoh ball. He brings

me the mushroom-and-barley. Then I complain. He gets a chance to say 'Don't make such a deal from it' and I get my mushroom-and-barley soup. It's what they call in the Science section a symbiotic relationship."

"So far, you're doing pretty well. It's not overwhelmingly believable."

"Here comes the good part. I am sitting there eating my mushroom-and-barley soup. The waiter is positively glowing because I'm eating it even though I very clearly ordered matzoh ball soup. I'm in a good mood because I figure that while I'm sitting there some poor son of a bitch is listening to Milt Silvers talk about how he got this really wacky idea to take his summer vacation in Jersey City. When who do I see—or whom do I see, if you want to be that way—walking past Hymie's?"

"Whom?"

"Ralph Holbrook. Syracuse Smiley. King of the Shmucks."

"I don't believe it."

"What'd I tell you?"

"But Smiley thinks the Lower East Side is Forty-fourth and Madison."

"Precisely," Wolferman said. "Which is why when I saw the Smiley One walk past, I jumped up, left the waiter the fifteen cent tip I always leave him so he has the opportunity to shout 'shnorrer' and 'paskudnyak' at me, dashed out the door, and started following Syracuse Smiley like a goddamned spy. What I was hoping for, I don't mind telling you, was to find him behind the pickle barrels at Guss's, fondling the private parts of Pete Smithers. Also, you know my theory that he's been nosing around trying to find his own reporting triumph so Towndsend'll forget that he started life as a ribbon clerk."

"So?" Becker said. "Then what happened?" He was as eager as Wolferman to find some way to embarrass Holbrook, even though he had difficulty imagining any embarrassment severe enough to stop what seemed to be Holbrook's inexorable progress toward taking over the magazine and making their lives unbearable.

"Well, I followed him down Houston Street—past Russ & Daughters and Moishe's and those places. He turned downtown at Essex, and then, around Rivington, he stopped at the door of a little cafe. He looked up and down the street—fortunately, I was standing behind a rack of coats on the sidewalk in front of one of those places that specializes in fleecing Puerto Ricans—and then he went in. He sat down at a table for two. The girl was already there."

"And?"

"And what?"

"And what-do-you-think? Who was it?"

"I don't know," Wolferman said. He shook his head from side to side sadly—an ace who had let the German fighter get away, a place-kicker who had missed from the fifteen-yard line.

"But how could you not know?" Becker said. "You know everybody at the magazine."

"That's what I'm telling you," Wolferman said. "She doesn't work here. I never saw her before."

"What did she look like?"

"Kind of ordinary," Wolferman said. "Although, I must say, she had a nice set of whatchamacallits."

Becker was truly disappointed. It was the first time

one of Wolferman's stories had failed to pin a name on a body. With potentially the most interesting and valuable morsel of his career within his reach, Wolferman had, for the first time ever, not recognized the girl. All he knew was that she had a nice set of—Jesus! Fred Becker said to himself. Mary Jane Wheeler!

Wednesday

17 He had been silly thinking that Mary Jane Wheeler was the woman Wolferman had spotted with Syracuse Smiley. That, at least, was what Becker told himself as the IRT local left the Eighteenth Street station on its way uptown. The problem, Becker thought, was that he was beginning to get the plot of his Washington novel mixed up with real life. In the novel, it might very well be true that the agent-in-place for the antiabortion lobby disappears through the efforts of those who see their political interests served by a trip to a willing and discrete gynecologist; in real life, Mary Jane Wheeler was probably on a confidential trip to Cleveland to iron out interethnic problems between the Latvians and the Slovaks. In the novel, it might make sense to have the Mary Jane character leak the news of the pregnancy to some reporter, but in real life Mary Jane Wheeler obviously didn't even know Ralph Holbrook. Becker might have managed to calm himself down completely by the Twenty-third Street station except for one sudden realization: Mary Jane Wheeler did know Fred Becker. That was real life. Why couldn't she be leaking the word to him through the Rug

Merchant? Why couldn't she be an agent-in-place for the antiabortion lobby or even the President's mistress? Why couldn't the forces desperate to hide the First Lady's pregnancy have done Mary Jane Wheeler some harm? Where was she? Where was the Rug Merchant?

Becker's farm belt friend, Duane Williams, had phoned from Washington that morning to say that, as far as he could tell, there had been nothing amiss in the First Lady's schedule except that a couple of engagements had been canceled over the weekend because of a slight case of flu. Could the flu have been a cover for some other medical interlude? Could Mary Jane Wheeler have found out? Becker found himself glancing at his fellow passengers—having suddenly considered the possibility that somebody might be following him. A heavyset man across the aisle looked up from the *Daily News*. He was wearing a plaid shirt and a baseball cap. Becker immediately looked away. Would an FBI man be dressed that way? Becker had always imagined FBI men as tidy types who had gone to Fordham and still wore stiff white collars. He glanced at the man again—and again met his eyes. Becker looked down. The man got up and walked toward him, swaying with the movement of the car. Becker tried to look away, but the man came close and stared down at him ominously.

"You try any queer stuff, buddy," the man said, "you're going to get used to wipe the floor with." Then he went back to his seat.

Becker sighed in relief, and opened his briefcase. The first of the correspondent files on the two-thirds stockings story had come in just before he left the office Tuesday afternoon, and he had shoved them into his briefcase to read on the subway. The first one he picked up was from Al Shackleford, the Cleveland stringer, who had two kids just entering college and was known for being able to find a lengthy example of any trend he was asked to look for. "Two-thirds stockings seem to be shaking up at least two-thirds of Shaker Heights," it began. "Says a woman prominent in the arts here: 'I can't imagine what I used to see in the other third.' " Becker recognized the woman prominent in the arts. It was Shackleford's wife, Hedda. Most of Shackleford's quotes were from her, no matter what the story. Sometimes she was quoted as a woman prominent in the arts (she ran an annual potluck dinner held in Shaker Heights to benefit the woodwind section of the Cleveland Symphony) and sometimes as a "suburban matron" and sometimes as a "former high-school beauty queen" and occasionally, particularly in stories about fitness or nutrition, as "a still svelte mother of four."

By the time the subway reached Becker's stop, the White House had been replaced in his mind by warehouses full of two-thirds stockings. He walked into his office ready to try out a few lead sentences. Andy Wolferman was sitting on his desk.

Becker took off his jacket and hung it on a hook. "I assume you're here to fill me in on some voyage of discovery you took last night to Bay Ridge or Far Rockaway," he said.

"I'm afraid not, Frederic. I've sunk to the level of mere water fountain stuff. About you."

"Let me guess," Becker said. "I've been named the new Ottawa bureau chief and ass-freezer."

"Close," Wolferman said. "You're about to be phoned by Syracuse Smiley, King of the Shmucks, and told that you're finishing out the week in Medicine."

"But I thought Doc was feeling better."

"Relapse."

"What's the matter with him?"

"Pam says she isn't sure," Wolferman said. "But I understand the doctors on the case haven't ruled out diaper rash."

"Are you sure about all this?" Becker asked. "How can you know?"

The telephone on Becker's desk rang. Wolferman picked up the receiver and handed it to Becker.

"Ralph Holbrook here, Fred," the voice on the other end said. "How are you? How's the family?"

18 Fred Becker came around the corner toward Doc Kennedy's office—carrying his expandable file in one hand and his sport jacket in the other—and found himself face to face with Milt Silvers. Becker wondered if Silvers had been there for some time—waiting for an audience to come along, the way a python waits quietly for a rat.

"The deal on the London taxi is closed," Silvers said. "Of course, you should have heard my insurance man's voice when I called to switch the insurance over from the John Deere tractor. He thinks I'm a little unusual."

Becker had never figured out how to reply to Silvers in a way that did not provoke more stories. Usually, he just stood there nodding dumbly while using the Thai's concentration methods or glancing around for escape routes.

"One of the great advantages of a London taxi, of course, is that if you happen to have a unicycle, which I just happen to have, the unicycle will fit snugly in the luggage area right next to the driver. Of course, when your average New York traffic cop sees a London taxi drive by with a unicycle right. . . ."

Becker briefly considered pretending to have a heart attack.

". . . didn't know there was a law, officer, against transporting unicycles by taxi. I just wonder what Woody will say when I drive up in my taxi—"

"Maybe he'll just say, 'Grand Central, driver, and step on it,' " a voice said. Becker looked around and saw Pam Robinson standing at the door to Doc Kennedy's office. "Or maybe he'll say, 'Driver, follow that tractor.' "

"I don't have the tractor anymore, Pam," Silvers said. "You see, I found that parking a tractor in New York was a real hassle—all these people saying—"

"Sorry to grab Fred away," Pam said, taking Becker by the arm and pulling him toward the office, "but we've got some late queries that have to go out in the next ten minutes."

Becker found himself in Doc Kennedy's office, where he had spent some unhappy hours writing about insides. His short romance with Pam had taken place during a long, intestine-haunted stint in Medicine while Doc Kennedy was on leave-of-absence doing a book on preteen vasectomy. Greta had just walked out on him. During the final few weeks of their marriage, she had seemed totally engaged by multimedia communications; when he picked up the note she had left, he assumed it would accuse him of being willfully linear. It said, "I cannot live with a man who makes a joke of preservatives."

Becker had not been sorry to see Greta leave—particularly after she made it clear that her alimony demands would not include any claim to his rent-controlled apartment. She was philosophically opposed to the rent-control laws for reasons Becker could no longer remember. He was lonely, though, and Pam Robinson, under her chatter, had turned out to be lonely too. It was a pleasant enough interlude, even though it often seemed to him that Pam wasn't paying much attention. Once or twice, he felt the need to tell her that "Becks-babes" was not really the name he wanted to be called by the person he was in bed with. Andy Wolferman had run across them in a clam house in Hoboken. The next morning, he had stuck his head into Becker's office and said, for the first time, "I think you're going to believe this one."

Becker looked around the office. The bookcase was dominated by medical texts. The cabinet that other writers used for copy paper and supplies had been converted into what amounted to a medicine chest. Becker put his expandable file in the corner and sat down behind the desk. "Thanks for rescuing me," he said to Pam Robinson.

"Anything for an old pal."

"I don't suppose we really do have anything that has to be out in ten minutes."

"No. Also, you can quit looking so doomed. Switching the sex capital story over here means no kishkes for you—except, of course, for an internal sex organ or two."

"Things seem to be going my way," Becker said, barely suppressing a shudder at the thought of what he might have to write about the pancreas if Doc Kennedy's diaper rash lasted another week. "Next thing you know, Cyprus will sink into the sea."

"Paul already left for lunch, which means he might not be putting the subject with the predicate when he gets back," Pam said. "I can go over the list with you." Paul

Venery, the senior editor whose responsibilities included Medicine, was a former foreign correspondent who was three years from retirement. He often spent the middle two or three hours of the day at a saloon in the East Fifties where a lot of foreign correspondents, temporarily or permanently grounded, liked to spend their time recalling moments of history like "that time the wire-service man in Kinsasha almost got his ass shot off running back to save the only waiter in the Congo who knew how to make real martinis." Venery was known for not interfering much with writers—or with anybody else except someone who tried to interrupt his anecdote about the Chinese whorehouse in Pusan or the time the man from the *London Sunday Telegraph* had to face the Canadian ambassador to Singapore in, for complicated reasons, the clothes of a novitiate of a Belgian order of nuns.

Pam gave one copy of the Medicine story list to Becker and began going down another copy. "It starts, for your entertainment, with the sex change capital story."

Becker nodded. "Right up my alley."

"Which is apparently where the doctor's office is," Pam said. "We got the first take of Cravens' report just before you came over. It's mostly about how this doctor switched from holistic podiatry a few years ago, when the sex change business began to get hot. But there's also some good stuff about the town. It doesn't actually say 'Sex Change Capital of the World' at the city limits, the way I'm sure you all hoped it would. It says 'A Fine Place to Work and Live' on one side of town and 'City of Churches' on the other side. But there's some good stuff about how people in town are making a living off the thing—dancing instructors teaching former men to follow rather than lead in the fox trot, and that sort of thing. Also, they want to use some of the limestone they have left over from the old days to build a statue symbolizing their new industry, and there's some interesting discussion about what it should be a statue of."

She handed him a copy of a follow-up query sent to Cravens in Indianapolis. It said, "Is any of the other new industry you mention sex-change related or what? Were there any intermediate steps between holistic podiatry and sex change operations? Still not certain what you mean by the phrase 'things fall off.' "

"What's this left-handed dentists story?" Becker said, studying the list.

"I really don't know."

"You don't know?"

"It was scheduled a few weeks ago, when I wasn't here, and it was postponed before the file came in from the bureau, and nobody seems to remember whether it's an organization of left-handed dentists or something about how hard it is to be a left-handed dentist or about people being superstitious about left-handed dentists or what. We should know today or tomorrow. Then, we have this piece on the doctor in L.A. they call Dermatologist to the Stars. Wait a minute. Dermatologist to the Stars has been scratched. Oh my God! Did I say that—'Dermatologist to the Stars has been scratched'?"

"I'm afraid so," Becker said, laughing.

"Well, it's been canceled is what I mean. I forgot. He turns out to be under suspicion of being a coke-pusher to the stars, and Paul thinks we ought to wait until that clears up."

"Clears up? With regular washing and some sunshine?"

"I'm sorry I started this. Anyway, the only story we have besides the sex capital piece and the mysterious left-handed dentists is disc banks in Cincinnati."

"Disco banks!" Becker said. "But that came up in Lifestyle. What does it have to do with Medicine? Now that I think of it, what are disco banks? Does that mean banks that service discos or discos in bank lobbies or—"

"Neither of those, dummy. It's not disco banks; it's disc banks. Like the discs in your back."

"You mean like a blood bank or an organ bank?"

"Of course. There's no such thing as disco banks."

"There may be now. Lifestyle did a piece on them in March."

They both started laughing. Then neither of them said anything for a while. "How have you been?" Becker finally said.

"You mean since last time you saw me—yesterday?" Pam said.

"No, I mean—well—in general."

"In general, O.K.," Pam said. "And you?"

"O.K.," Becker said.

"You seem a bit subdued. Did Greta write you another letter accusing you of using too much copy paper or something?"

"No, I haven't heard from her in years," Becker said. The talk of the sex change doctor's previous career, in fact, had reminded him that one place he had always expected Greta to turn up was in the administration of a holistic health clinic. Becker tapped a pencil on Doc Kennedy's desk. Suddenly, he knew he was going to confide in Pam

Robinson. He had to tell somebody. He had felt close to Pam even before they had what Wolferman insisted on calling their "mini-thing." Also, she was the Medicine researcher. She might even have some factual knowledge that would be valuable to him in trying to decide what to do with the information he had—or in trying to decide whether or not what he had was really information.

"Pam," he said. "Can I talk to you sort of confidentially? I hate to put it that way, but it's something I haven't discussed with anybody, and it sort of has to be kept like that."

Pam Robinson got up, shut the door of Doc Kennedy's office, and then sat down again. "Shoot," she said.

"I have reason to believe that somebody might be pregnant, and that—"

"Jennifer Kanter," Pam said. "It's got to be Jennifer Kanter."

"Jennifer Kanter?"

"Jennifer Kanter. Third most attractive researcher in the Foreign Affairs section. Tied for third, really."

"What does Jennifer Kanter have to do with this?"

"I was thinking it might be Carol Goodenow. I've seen you sneaking glances in the direction of Carol Goodenow. But it couldn't be Carol Goodenow, because she couldn't bring herself to tell you she's pregnant. It would embarrass her to pieces. So it must be Jennifer Kanter—nice, if slightly hippy, Jennifer Kanter."

"That isn't what I'm talking about, Pam. Listen, can I really trust you?"

"Unless it's the Bombshell. If it's the Bombshell, you can't trust me. Otherwise, you can trust me."

"Pam, this doesn't have anything to do with me or

anybody around here. The person I'm talking about is the President's wife."

"The President of—"

Becker nodded. "The President of the United States. The Commander in Chief of the Army and Navy. The Leader of the Free World."

19 "The goddamned story won't write," Charlie Sayler said, in his customary monotone. They were gathered at the Bamboo Gardens for lunch. The day being Wednesday, a waiter had just delivered four white wine spritzers.

"Mine either," Bryan Murray said. "It won't write. I figured that as long as it wasn't going to write I might as well knock off a chapter or two of the prom program book, but I had to spend half the morning on the phone to Atlanta with Frank O'Hearn. He's still pissed off about a story we ran in Education last week on that governor down there firing the school commissioner. He said the story that finally ran didn't have anything at all to do with his file."

"Imagine that," Wolferman said. "Nothing to do with the file."

"It's the sort of thing that could eventually lead a person toward disenchantment," Sayler said.

"He goes on and on about how many pages he wrote explaining how this differed from the stock red-necked-governor - fires - school - commissioner - for - being - insuf-ficiently-bigoted story, and then that's what it ended up reading like in the magazine," Murray said. "I told him I was guilty only of oversimplifying his file almost beyond recognition. The real trouble came when Smithers, who had only skimmed O'Hearn's file, oversimplified my over-simplification, and then Woody, who hadn't read it at all, oversimplified Smithers' oversimplification."

"I have tried to explain to O'Hearn that there are certain natural laws," Sayler said. "Control over the story increases in inverse ratio to knowledge of what actually went on. If he wanted to have some power over what was in the magazine, he should have had the sense to stay away from the scene of the event."

"I finally got rid of O'Hearn, and then, of course, it turns out my story won't write. It just sits there, like a bowl of cold oatmeal."

"What're you working on?" Sayler asked, although he didn't sound very interested.

"Wild monkeys," Murray said.

"Wild monkeys?" Sayler said. He looked as close to surprised as he ever managed to look—an expression Andy Wolferman had compared to a basset hound at bay. "That's what I'm doing—wild monkeys."

Murray took a drink of his spritzer and put the glass down on the table carefully. "You're writing a story about wild monkeys?" he said.

Sayler nodded.

"Wild monkeys in Dahomey?"

"Those are the wild monkeys."

"Aren't all monkeys wild?" Wolferman asked. "I mean except monkeys who work for organ grinders and that crowd."

Neither Murray nor Sayler answered him. Becker stirred his drink.

"Well, we were about due for a wild monkey story," Wolferman said. "Two wild monkey stories would be even better, I think."

"I can't believe those dumb bastards have two of us writing the same story," Sayler said, shaking his head. "No, I take that back. I can believe it. I know that's what we all have in store for us between now and the time Syracuse Smiley hands us that gold watch. Years of writing monkey stories in concert."

"I'm going to let you write that wild monkey story," Murray said. "It'll cheer you up, Charlie."

"No, I couldn't do that to you, Bryan. As much as I want to write about the little fellows, it's really a Science story. So it's all yours."

"I'm not in Science this week," Murray said. "I'm in Foreign Affairs."

"Well, all the better. They're definitely foreign monkeys. These are not American monkeys we're talking about."

"Spring-BOK, Spring-BOK," Wolferman said. "Spring-BOK, Spring-BOK."

"It's your story, Charlie," Murray said. "And I'm going to be big about telling Thompson that. Definitely a National News story—policy implications toward the Third World, questions of whether the President's going to bring economic sanctions to bear against those wicked poachers."

"I understand Eisen's hired a seaplane to get Gessler into where the monkeys are," Wolferman said. "Two seaplanes, actually. A seaplane and a back-up seaplane."

"One of us will have written the story from the clips long before Gessler gets in and out of there," Murray said.

"Maybe both of you," Wolferman said. "But they needed something for the Editor's Note, and Gessler flying into monkeyland on two seaplanes seemed just the ticket."

"Dumb bastards," Sayler said again. "If we hadn't happened to have lunch together, we both would have broken our asses trying to write about wild monkeys. Well, at least one of us will be sprung."

"I lose either way," Murray said. "I've also got Cyprus this week. That cheer you up, Fred?"

Becker nodded, and held up his drink in a silent toast—but he was not, in fact, cheered up. Telling Pam Robinson everything had not, as it turned out, lifted a great burden from his shoulders. After a long talk, Pam had suggested that he say nothing to anybody else for a couple of days, then try Mary Jane Wheeler again. It was the sort of advice he would ordinarily have been happy to get—there was nothing more comforting, he always believed, than to be told by a thoughtful adviser that inaction was the wisest course to pursue—but he was eager to find out at least whether Wentzell's story was true, even if he then retreated to inaction rather than deciding what to do about it. Also, he was concerned about Mary Jane Wheeler. The only thing keeping him from panic about what might have happened to her, he decided, was the belief that the Rug Merchant was not simply too loony to be a bonafide spy but too loony even to cause anybody any real danger.

"Woody's finally going to get briefed by the President," Wolferman said. "Tomorrow morning."

"Well, I'm sure he'll address the wild monkey issue head-on," Sayler said.

"He's taking Syracuse Smiley with him," Wolferman said.

There was silence at the table for a while—everyone there obviously reflecting on the implication of Ralph Holbrook's having been chosen to make the sort of trip a future managing editor might be chosen to make.

"I suppose if Syracuse Smiley takes over he'll have to find someone else to run the charity drive," Murray said. "Although I can't imagine anyone else doing it with that style that so successfully blends Norman Vincent Peale with Mussolini."

Nobody said anything for a while. "Someone else will have to step in as the smiling people-shifter," Wolferman said. "A little grin for a six-month sentence to the Business section. A chuckle for a few winters in Ottawa."

"He'll be there to hand us the gold watches," Sayler said.

They stared at their drinks for a while. Then Wolferman beckoned the waiter. "We're working on the Malay calendar this week, Ching, my man," he said. "Better change these spritzers to four Scotches."

20 Woody Fenton and Ralph Holbrook flew to Washington on the last air shuttle Wednesday night. Their appointment at the White House was early Thursday morning, giving them time to return to New York for the final editing and closing of the magazine. On the shuttle, Fenton quickly became engrossed in the Eastern Airlines flight magazine—smiling contentedly as he read. Ralph Holbrook was fingering the pipe in his pocket—impatient to give it a try but wary of the airlines' rule against pipe smoking. He often glanced across the aisle at a man who looked tantalizingly familiar—an unprepossessing-looking man with thick glasses and a fringe of gray hair.

A limousine dispatched by the Washington bureau picked them up at National Airport and delivered them to the Hay-Adams Hotel, just across Lafayette Square from the White House. As they approached the registration desk, Holbrook again saw the man who had been sitting across the aisle on the shuttle. He was registering for a room. Holbrook edged around to get a peek at the name on the registration card, but even before he read it he realized who the man was—Emmanual Froelich, the Disco Doc, Middle of the Week Manny.

The clerk scribbled a couple of numbers on the doctor's registration card, and then turned to the key board. "Oh, Dr. Froelich," he said, pulling a small envelope out of the box along with the key. "This was left for you." Holbrook managed to get a look at the envelope. The return address, printed in blue, was just three words: "The White House."

In the elevator, Holbrook said to Fenton, "Woody, as important as the wild monkey issue is, I think there's another subject we might explore with the President if we get an opportunity after the Middle East briefing."

"What's that, Ralph?"

With a gesture of his head, Holbrook indicated the bellhop, who was standing stiffly in front of them. "Maybe I'll just stop by your room for a minute, Woody."

In Fenton's room, the bellhop flipped on the light, arranged Fenton's suitcase on a stand, and opened the curtains—revealing a view of the White House, dramatically illuminated across the square. Explaining that he would carry his own bag to his room, Holbrook dismissed the bellhop with a tip and immediately began talking to Woody Fenton in a low voice. The bellhop thanked Holbrook and left—but not before he heard Woody Fenton say, in a loud voice, "Golly!"

Thursday

21 It was a clear, bright morning. A bum who was making his way across Lafayette Square seemed to be moving with some spring in his step. Fenton and Holbrook had decided to walk across the square to the White House, rather than be delivered by the limousine. As they walked, they discussed how long they might have to listen to a briefing on the Middle East, a subject they both found tedious, before they had an opportunity to ask some questions of their own. In story conferences concerning the Middle East, Fenton's voice changed from a bored monotone only when he spoke of a dinner party he once attended at the home of the Israeli ambassador— where a famous movie actress had so impressed him with her beauty and her informed questions about what it was like to edit a great national newsmagazine that he had decided to put her picture on the cover.

"It could be, of course, that the doctor is just at the White House attending some sort of conference," Fenton said.

"Of course, that could be, Woody," Holbrook said.

"Still, added to what I've been able to find out from my other sources. . . ."

They had just come out of Lafayette Square, about to cross Pennsylvania Avenue, when an ambulance, going very slowly, approached them from the direction of the White House gate. As it passed, the man sitting in the passenger seat put on a hat and lowered it over his eyes. As he did so, though, Ralph Holbrook and Woody Fenton both got a good look at his face. It was Emmanual Froelich.

The President was standing next to the fireplace in one of the small studies on the second floor of the White House. He leaned against the mantlepiece casually, holding a cup of coffee, which he sipped occasionally. Two of his aides sat in straight chairs near the wall. One of them took notes. Holbrook and Fenton sat on a couch in front of the fireplace. Holbrook had already failed in his first attempt to acquire a White House matchbook: he had filled his pipe, patted his pocket as if to locate his matches, and suddenly found one of the aides at his side holding a lighter whose flames shot deep into the pipe's bowl.

"In answer to your question, Mr. Fenton," the President was saying, "I see no reason to believe that our plans for bringing peace to this area are any threat at all to the Sinai wild goat."

"I know the Israeli prime minister is quite interested in animals personally," Fenton said.

"Yes, I believe he told me he had a cat," the President said.

"Two cats," Fenton said.

"Is that right?" the President said.

"Yes sir," one of the aides snapped. "Two at our last report, sir."

"Well, good," the President said.

There was a moment or two of silence.

"A Persian and an Abyssinian," Fenton said. "The Persian has a Persian name and the Abyssinian has an Abyssinian name. I met them."

"I didn't know there were any Abyssinian names left," the President said.

"Apparently so."

"Well, fine," the President said. He took a sip of his coffee. "At any rate, I think I can put your mind at rest about the Sinai wild goat. Wouldn't you say so, Perkins?"

"Yes sir, Mr. President," one of the aides said.

"Well, swell," Fenton said. "That's dandy."

"Just between us," the President said, "the Egyptian foreign minister happens to have a lady friend who is particularly fond of the Sinai wild goat herd."

"Is that right?" Fenton said.

The President smiled and nodded. "Just between us, of course."

"Of course," Fenton said.

There was silence in the room. The President sipped his coffee. Woody Fenton took a pipe from his pocket and, without lighting it, began to puff away. It burned steadily.

"Hope your wife is feeling better, Mr. President," Holbrook said. "She was a bit under the weather last time we were here."

"Oh, yes, thanks, she's fine now," the President said. "Sorry we had to put that meeting off after you had come all the way down here."

"What was the problem?" Holbrook said. "If I may ask."

"Oh, just some sort of intestinal flu," the President said.

"Just the flu?"

"Yes, the flu," the President said, beginning to sound rather impatient with the line of questioning. Perkins shifted in his chair, as if thinking about rising.

"No other problems?" Holbrook persisted.

The President looked puzzled. "I'm afraid I don't understand what you're getting at, Mr. Holbrook," he said.

"Well, for instance, Mr. President, we just saw an ambulance that seemed to be coming from here, with a very well known gynecologist in it."

"A gynecologist injured here?" the President said, turning to his aides. "I'm afraid I don't understand."

Holbrook was trying to get his pipe going again with some furious puffing, but no smoke emerged. The aide who had previously offered his lighter did not move. Holbrook looked around, but there were no matches in sight. Finally, he withdrew the pipe from his mouth, took a deep breath, and said, "Mr. President, may I ask you—on a deep background basis at this point if you wish—is the First Lady, or has she recently been, pregnant?"

The President looked incredulously at Holbrook. Then he turned to Fenton. "I was told, Mr. Fenton," he said, "that you had some interest in the issue of wild monkeys in Dahomey."

Before Fenton could reply, Holbrook said, "Because, Mr. President, if our exclusive on this is protected—and I'm speaking for Mr. Fenton here—we would certainly be willing to talk about the sort of approach to the story that might be the most dignified, and may I say in that regard—"

"This is off the subject of wild monkeys," the President said to Fenton.

Fenton seemed unable to speak. He was still smiling—the smile that his face wore at rest—and he was puffing rapidly on his pipe. One large puff of white smoke after another emerged from the bowl. Holbrook had taken out a thin notebook that said "Reporter's Notebook" on the front, and had, with an exaggerated gesture, flipped it open and poised a pen over the first page.

"Certain information has come to our attention, sir," Holbrook said. "With all respect, I have to say that it indicates the strong possibility that the First Lady might be, well, with child, or might have, in a matter of speaking, terminated the pregnancy."

There was silence in the room. The presidential aide who had been taking notes stopped writing.

"Some information that apparently didn't come to your attention is the following," the President said, still addressing Woody Fenton, who was barely visible in the smoky haze around him. "My wife had a hysterectomy four and a half years ago at New York Hospital. Perkins here can show you the hospital report, if that's the sort of thing that interests you."

Fenton looked at Ralph Holbrook. Holbrook started puffing on his pipe, to no avail. "Golly," Fenton finally said. "Gosh! Holy Smoke! Jumping Jehoshaphat! Jumping Goddamn Jehoshaphat!"

The President put his coffee cup on the mantlepiece.

Perkins and the other aide stood up. "I'm certain you gentlemen understand that the President has a busy morning," Perkins said.

Fenton and Holbrook stood up—Fenton's head emerging clearly for the first time from the cloud of pipe smoke.

"I'm afraid, in fact, I might be rather busy for the rest of my term," the President said. "It is rather time-consuming, being the Chief of State and Commander in Chief of the Armed Forces, and all. I'm sure Perkins here can help you with any questions you may have in the future. He's one of our best men on beasts of the field." The President walked toward the door, and then turned once more to Fenton. "You forgot Gloryosky Zero," he said, and walked out of the room.

22 Late Thursday morning, Becker tried to start on the left-handed dentists story, even though the file from the bureau was still not in. The sex change capital story was already on Paul Venery's desk, the product of a long Wednesday evening Becker had spent at the office. When Wednesday afternoon had come and gone with no sign of the left-handed dentists report, Pam had sent a wire to the Chicago bureau chief reminding him that all back-of-the-book files were supposed to be in by Wednesday morning, and the Chicago bureau chief had replied that he had never heard of the left-handed dentists story. He suggested that it might have originated in the Boston bureau or the Los Angeles bureau. Neither had heard of it. Pam had immediately sent a roundup query to all bureaus which began, "Need soonest for late-breaking Medicine story on left-handed dentists. . . ." So far, there had been no replies.

Lacking any information about the story beyond its subject, Becker was going on the assumption that it had something to do with the inconvenience or additional equipment expense left-handed dentists suffered. He was toying with a first sentence that began "Ask a left-handed schoolboy how his sinistral tendencies affect his career choices, and he would probably say that the paucity of left-handed shortstops. . . ." He pulled the paper out of his typewriter and threw it away. He rolled in another piece of copy paper and started again: "Is being approached from the left by a drill much more terrifying for the average dental patient than being approached from the right?" He threw that one away, and began, "Experts have long assumed that if the question of left-right orientation were raised under provisions of the federal fair employment act, it would be raised in the field of dentistry." He threw that one away, too. He rolled a fresh piece of paper into the typewriter and stared at it for a while.

Andy Wolferman stuck his head in the door. "You better sit down for this one," he said.

"I'm already sitting down."

"Well, scrunch into the chair a little, then, because this one will reduce you to jelly. This is water fountain stuff that rises above the form."

Becker sat back, put both arms on the arms of his chair, and said, "I'm ready. Hit me with it."

"Who do you think will be named in a memo from Woody this afternoon as the new chief of our Ottawa bureau, according to reliable sources?"

"How many guesses do I get?"

"One hundred and thirteen."

"Why one hundred and thirteen?"

"Because there are one hundred and fourteen people on the staff, and you know perfectly well that Paul Venery's been persona non grata in Canada since the unfortunate incident he and the Agence France Presse man were involved in at the governor-general's reception. So that leaves one hundred thirteen eligibles."

"In that case, I give up."

"Ralph Holbrook."

"Ralph Holbrook!"

"If you don't recognize him by that name," Wolferman said, "I might say that we are talking about the person also known as Syracuse Smiley, just plain Smiley, the Smiley One, King of the Shmucks, and the Shithead."

"Ottawa!"

"Ottawa," Wolferman said. "Cold Ottawa. Boring Ottawa. Never in the magazine Ottawa. Perfect place for King of the Shmucks Ottawa."

"But why?" Becker said. "How?"

"Nobody can read Woody's mind, of course," Wolferman said. "Not all that many people can find Woody's mind. However, if I had to guess, I would say that Smiley is going to be sent to Ottawa because Woody is no longer likely to be invited back to the White House and that Woody is no longer likely to be invited back to the White House because Syracuse Smiley offended the Leader of the Free World and made a complete ass out of himself by confronting the President with the lunatic notion that the First Lady was pregnant."

Becker and Wolferman looked at each other in silence. Charlie Sayler appeared in the doorway. Finally, Becker said, "What made him think that the First Lady was pregnant?"

"Why don't we discuss it at lunch?" Wolferman said.

Becker grabbed his jacket, and they started out the door. "Is Rocco talking to Milt?" he asked automatically.

"I'm afraid Rocco has resigned that position," Wolferman said. "Milt talked to him for an hour and a half yesterday about all the zany colors he might paint the London taxi. When we got back from the Gardens, they were still on the phone from the call covering us to the elevator. Rocco says he'd rather give up the ponies than go through that again."

Bryan Murray fell into step with them. "Let's take a chance," he said. "Maybe Milt put himself to sleep."

Silvers was not in his office. They made it safely down the elevator and set off for the Bamboo Gardens. They walked in silence. Becker had found Wolferman's news almost too astounding to theorize about. Had there been another leak at the White House which somehow found its way to Holbrook? Did this mean that the President's wife was not, in fact, pregnant? How did anybody know with such certainty? Just inside the door of the Bamboo Gardens, Milt Silvers was waiting for them.

"Hi," he said. "I thought I might run into you guys. I was just out talking to some of those car customizers on the West Side about what color to paint my taxi. This one guy said, 'fleet or independent,' and I said 'London,' so he kind of jumped back and—"

"Milt," Wolferman said, holding up five fingers as they walked to their table. "I'd love to hear that painting story. Rocco tells me it's a riot. Zany in the extreme. The problem is this: there's something pretty important we have to discuss at lunch today, so maybe we can put off the taxi thing for a while."

"Well, sure, Andy," Silvers said, looking a bit hurt.

"We'd be happy to have you join us, though," Becker said.

They settled themselves in at their usual table. Nobody said anything until the waiter brought the drinks—although Milt Silvers looked as if he wanted to.

"Well," Becker said. "Tell me about the President's wife."

"Boy," Milt Silvers said. "I'll never forget the time when I was in the Washington bureau and we were all invited to that big reception they have on the White House lawn in the spring, and I happened to have my iguana at the time—Luis Borges was his name—and when Luis Borges and I—"

"Milt," Wolferman said. "We can't hear about it now."

"I've got to get back to the monkeys pretty quick," Sayler said.

"Not a word about Luis Borges or your cheetah or your walking catfish," Wolferman said. "O.K.?"

Silvers shrugged, and fell silent.

"You see," Becker said. "I happened to hear the same story—I mean about the President's wife."

"I know," Wolferman said.

"How do you know?"

"Because I leaked it to you," Wolferman said. "Or I should really say we leaked it to you, because there are unnamed parties who qualify as unindicted co-conspirators."

"But I heard it from Leonard Wentzell."

"You have just named one of the unnamed parties."

"But why? What is all this? Why would you want Leonard Wentzell to tell me that the President's wife was pregnant."

"Because she wasn't," Wolferman said. "She just had the flu."

Becker could feel himself flush with anger. "Do you

mean you planted a phony story so I could break it and make a complete fool out of myself, but Smiley just happened to get there first?"

"Of course not, Fred," Wolferman said. "Smiley was the fool we had in mind at the start. You know my theory that he's been on the lookout for some big scoop that would make Woody and Towndsend forget that his background is in clerking rather than reporting. And we figured the devious little bastard would have real faith only in a story he stole from someone else."

"But he couldn't have stolen it from me," Becker said. "He'd be the last person I'd tell anything to. You know that. In fact, I haven't told anybody, at least not until yesterday morning, and then I—"

Wolferman was nodding something that looked ominously like Wentzell's knowing nod.

"Pam and Smiley?" Becker said.

Wolferman nodded what was definitely a knowing nod.

Becker raised his hand above his head to signal for five more drinks. "Start from the beginning," he said.

Wolferman explained how he had conspired to have Wentzell plant the story, and how he had then, on the theory that Becker would feel the need to confide in someone, arranged to make Pam Robinson the one to confide in—having known, from a chance observation at the jai alai fronton near Bridgeport, that Pam and Smiley were part of the eternal statistic.

"You mean Doc isn't really sick?"

"Even less sick than he is when he's sick," Wolferman said. "He was a quick volunteer—partly because he despises

Syracuse Smiley, of course, and partly, I'm afraid, because he thought it was pancreas week in the Medicine section. He'll recover today."

"But Mary Jane Wheeler. Where has she been?"

"In her office, interethnicing," Wolferman said. "She told her secretary to be very guarded if you called because you had thrown a root beer down the front of her dress in high school and you might still be subject to bizarre acts of violence."

"Did you try to hint to me that it was Mary Jane with Smiley on the Lower East Side, saying that she had a big pair of whatzits?"

"I'm afraid so."

"But why? What did that have to do with anything?"

"Damned if I know," Wolferman said. "That was Wentzell's idea. He said it would increase your anxiety about Mary Jane and also keep you from guessing that Pam was the one seeing Smiley—since, if I may say so with no criticism intended, Pam's whatzits aren't all that big. It all seemed pretty overcomplicated to me, but Wentzell insisted it was based on some psychological reinforcement techniques perfected by the Portuguese secret police in Mozambique. Boy, is he full of shit sometimes!"

"But why was Smiley so sure that what he stole from me was true?" Becker said. "I told Pam I really didn't know."

Wolferman explained a few "confirming touches" the conspirators had arranged—the participation of Emmanual Froelich, for instance. Still irritated about Holbrook's having caused him to miss two racing weekends with the offensive drophead, Froelich had been willing to go to Washington, flash an envelope from the White House, and even ride in an ambulance that Holbrook assumed was coming from the White House simply because it approached from that direction. When Marvin Rappaport, the Washington bureau chief, was asked by Holbrook to see if there had been anything unusual about the First Lady's schedule, Wolferman said, he reported only that someone else had been nosing around the same subject.

Becker nodded. "A guy I asked to," he said.

"Not having much experience in these matters," Wolferman said, "the Smiling One put two and two together and got zapped."

"Wait a minute," Becker said. "How do you know the President's wife isn't pregnant after all?"

"Because she had a hysterectomy four and a half years ago. They kept it secret—Christ knows why; maybe he was worried about losing the pro-uterus vote—but the First Lady confessed it to Mary Jane between tree dedications, and Mary Jane told Wentzell, and Wentzell told me." Mary Jane Wheeler had forgiven Wentzell for the root beer incident, Wolferman explained, and they had become a quiet item in Washington—quiet because Mary Jane was not certain how her career would be affected if it became public that she was seeing a man who implied that he was in the pay of any number of foreign intelligence operations. Wolferman had come across them in a crab cake stand on the Eastern Shore of Maryland, and there the plot was hatched.

The waiter came up, and Wolferman said, "How about two mu-shus, a nineteen, fried dumplings, and lo mein with the glop of the day?" Nobody answered, since Wolferman was writing down the order as he spoke and handed it to the waiter the moment he finished.

The process of piecing together the facts of the conspiracy had calmed Becker down a bit, but he again found himself growing angry. It was irritating that Leonard Wentzell had indeed turned out to be a secret agent of sorts—covertly manipulating the friends of his childhood. It was even more irritating to have been used as a sort of passive conduit in the plot. Becker was silent for a while. He thought about the plans that had gone through his head since the Rug Merchant told him the President's wife was pregnant—the methods of breaking the story, the possibility of a blockbuster novel. He was about to say "you used me" when it occurred to him that he had uttered that line in a play in college. On the other hand, it was appropriate—unlike in the play in college. "You used me," he said.

"But in a good cause," Wolferman said.

"But that's just it," Becker said. "The cause was just internal crap at the magazine. You involved the President of the United States, the—the—"

"Leader of the Free World?"

"Right. The Leader of the Free World. Just for water fountain stuff."

"You are looking at desperate men," Charlie Sayler said.

"If it hadn't worked out just right—and you were awfully damn lucky—the story could have ended up in the magazine."

"Well, the way we look at it," Wolferman said. "People leak stories in Washington all the time for their own selfish reasons. This time, it was for our own selfish reasons. We ought to get a turn now and then."

The waiter showed up with what might have been nineteen and what might have been lo mein with the glop of the day. They all started eating. Becker had to admit that he was relieved at being saved from Syracuse Smiley— grateful, even. The magazine under Smiley would have been unbearable. Becker would have been permanently wedded to the ancient battle between Greek and Turk. Once the benign power of Woody Fenton no longer existed, Holbrook might have done anything. Maybe he would have instituted a dress code. Maybe he would have held Troop Information and Education lectures. However sneaky Wolferman's plot had been, it was obviously skillful—a great improvement on his palpably silly rhinoceros head plot. Becker found himself viewing the entire affair with some admiration.

"Not a bad scheme," he said.

Wolferman beamed. Sayler nearly managed a smile.

"Where in the hell did you manage to get hold of an ambulance?" Becker asked.

Milt Silvers looked up, obviously intent on speaking no matter what stricture had been imposed. "I had one," he said.

23

Becker stared at the typewriter. The two-thirds stockings story was not going well. He was accustomed to "writing around" facts that didn't happen to be available or ambiguities that were too complicated to resolve, but the files on two-thirds stockings conflicted in a way that tried his skills. As he had predicted to Carol Goodenow, a number of bureaus and stringers provided lengthy reports about the popularity of two-thirds stockings, but there was some disagreement about whether the phenomenon consisted of stockings two-thirds up the leg or two-thirds of the way to the knee or just two-thirds of a stocking. Sicola, the originator of the suggestion, had indeed found a California designer who took credit for the craze, but the interview with him—an interview crammed with phrases like "the allure of the partial" and "an almost mannerist tension of missingness"—gave no indication at all of what a two-thirds stocking might look like. Becker realized that the issue would have to be resolved if he was going to avoid spending the evening at his desk. He decided that two-thirds stockings went two-thirds of the way up the leg.

The two-thirds stockings story appeared to be the only story that was going to cause him much trouble. The obscene topiary story had already been initialed by both Pete Smithers and Woody Fenton. Smithers had gone straight for the decoy sentences and had let the rest of the story stand pretty much as written. A first-rate file was in from San Francisco on the story about drowning in hot-tubs. In just the first quick reading of it, Becker had spotted the quotation that could serve as the last line of the story—a quotation from a funeral eulogy by an Open World Unitarian minister, who said, "And so we say goodbye to our beloved Josh, in touch with his body at last."

Becker was relieved to be out of Medicine. He would have to see Pam sooner or later, of course, but if they managed to put it off until much later they might be able to avoid talking about what had happened that week. He didn't feel up to confronting Pam with her betrayal of confidence. He didn't feel up to discussing her relationship with Syracuse Smiley. He certainly didn't feel up to writing about the pancreas. The sex change story had been switched to the Business section, and Doc Kennedy, already suffering from pains in the lower abdomen, was only now beginning to wrestle with the explanation of how enzymes from the pancreas find their way about the body.

The telephone rang, and Becker, thankful for the interruption, picked it up. Dick Chiles greeted him cheerfully.

"How'd things go at your accountant's?" Becker asked, after Holbrook's new assignment to Ottawa had been discussed.

"He says I should become a tax shelter."

"Get a tax shelter?"

"No, become a tax shelter," Chiles said. "I already have too many tax shelters. This is some deal where a lot of dentists from California get together and buy the Kurdish language rights to my books, and then write it off when the Kurds don't take up the option. Something like that. Serbo-Croatian movie rights—that sort of thing. I found it rather intriguing, but then I realized I could never stand the thought of a bunch of dentists sitting around the swimming pool comparing me to cattle ranches and shrimp boat operations. Anyway, that's not why I called. I heard some gossip about your book in Antonio's today at lunch."

"Who'd you have lunch with?"

"My editor."

"What'd he have to say about it?"

"He wasn't the one I heard the gossip from."

"Oh. Who was it?"

"How the hell am I supposed to know? The guy was four or five tables away. Over by the kitchen. He must not be very important, now that I think of it—being over by the kitchen. But sometimes people who aren't very important know things that are very important. Anyway, he asked whoever he was having lunch with if he had heard of an auction coming up on a blockbuster White House novel that's supposed to be truly big bucks."

"How do you know it's my novel they were talking about?"

"Because they said the auction floor was going to be a hundred and fifty thousand."

"But we were talking about a hundred for mine," Becker said.

"Of course. And that was two days ago. That's the whole point of starting it at Antonio's. It always tends to go up about twenty-five percent a day. I think you're doing O.K. Remember, whenever you're tempted to cut, add a few paragraphs. They pay by the pound."

Becker thanked Chiles and hung up. The novel, he knew, was still possible. Fenton and Holbrook and the White House people all had reason to keep quiet about what had happened at the briefing, and Wolferman's conspirators were sworn to silence. Since lunch, Becker had even thought of a new twist for the plot. Weston, the devious and unkempt presidential counsel, purposely floats a rumor about the First Lady's having had an abortion, knowing that it will be picked up and spread around by the President's political opponents. The President is down in the polls; his opponents believe that the abortion rumor will finish him off. Just as that seems to be happening, the trap is sprung. The President goes on national television to confront the rumors head-on—armed with the hospital records of his wife's hysterectomy and with a simple, but eloquent, speech written by Rod Baxter ("In my heart, I feel not anger but sadness that, whatever sincere differences exist between Americans on this most serious matter, there are those among us who would stain the sacred institution of motherhood with their mud-slinging."). The backlash carries the President back into office for a second term. The speech makes Baxter a hero in the White House, but at the party celebrating the scheme's success he announces his resignation—dramatically, in the manner of the lawyer at the celebration following the *Caine Mutiny* trial—and says he wants nothing to do with people who would use an unborn baby to serve their own selfish ends. Thinking about the scene, Becker realized for the first time that there was no unborn baby involved; the First Lady had not, in fact, been pregnant. He would have to think of another reason for Baxter to drop his White House pass on the President's desk and walk out of the Oval Office—having no future in mind except to return to the simple quiet of his rent-controlled apartment.

Even if he did start working on his book during weekends and evenings and the first couple of quiet days of the workweek, Becker realized, he no longer thought of a blockbuster novel as a way to leave the magazine forever. He would probably stick around, even if Syracuse Smiley somehow managed to engineer a return to power, like some wicked prince who returns to England in a Hollywood film about medieval knights. ("He'll find Towndsend some nearly extinct caribou up there," Charlie Sayler had said, reverting to pessimism toward the end of lunch. "Mark my word.") Working so closely with the same people week after week was, as Andy Wolferman often said, "like being snowed in all winter in a village populated by particularly neurotic villagers," but Becker had become accustomed to the village. He realized that he, too, might have been willing to involve the White House in a plot to keep Syracuse Smiley from taking over. He had long taken it for granted that the internal goings on at the magazine were more important than the events the magazine wrote about. Sometimes he daydreamed about a magazine that dealt with the magazine—a Science story about the mathematical probability of Wolferman running across that many couples, a Medicine story about Doc Kennedy's sympathetic illnesses, a color picture spread of the Bombshell. He would do the story on Milt Silvers himself—for Lifestyle, or perhaps Behavior. Before that, though, he would have to conquer the two-thirds stockings story. He put a fresh piece of copy paper in his typewriter.

Friday

24 It was almost eleven on Friday morning. Fred Becker and Carol Goodenow had been checking the Lifestyle stories for an hour. As a researcher, Carol was particularly conscientious about making certain that there was some acceptable source for every fact presented in the story. Becker, trying to preserve his prose, was in a position Wolferman often compared to trying to protect a baby while a crazed woman clawed at it. Carol often cried on Fridays, but she seemed pretty well in control as she went through the hot-tub story Becker had finished the night before.

"I don't think you can say here 'from San Jose to Monterey,' " she was saying.

"They rhyme," Becker said.

"I know they rhyme, but it's misleading. San Jose and Monterey are both south of San Francisco, and, according to my calculations, seventy-eight percent of the drownings we're talking about happened in Marin County, north of San Francisco. Also, I can't check that there has ever been an authenticated hot-tub drowning in Monterey."

"I distinctly remember somebody in Muller's report being taken to the hospital in Monterey."

"Yes, but the incident actually happened in Carmel, not Monterey. Also, it wasn't a drowning. Somebody who didn't change the water in his hot-tub for a long time finally got hepatitis."

They discussed the problem for another fifteen minutes. Finally, they agreed on "from Salinas to Bolinas"— even though Carol said Salinas was not the sort of place that had a lot of hot-tubs and Becker said that he resented having to settle for an inferior rhyme simply because of a checking detail he considered nit-picking.

"How about the dirty bushes story?" Becker said.

Carol blushed.

"There's nothing really dirty the way I wrote it," Becker said, trying to reassure her.

"I just thought it might be upsetting for you—I mean the mention of Greta," Carol said.

"What mention of Greta?"

"In Art Fletcher's update report from Phoenix. You mean you didn't see it?"

"I never read anything that comes in after the story's O.K.'d. You know that."

Carol took a deep breath. "Greta is the social director of the Pillow Talk Arms Singles Complex in Phoenix," she said. "She's in Art's report."

"The Greta I was married to?"

Carol nodded.

Becker sank back in his chair. "Are you sure?"

"Apparently she mentioned you to Art. She's quoted in the file. She says—," Carol flipped through some of the pages in a folder she was carrying. "She says, 'There was a great bunch of guys and gals here even before we hired Lance Matthews as our resident topiarist. But they really came a-runnin' when they heard what fun things Lance was doing with the bushes.' "

"She said that?"

Carol nodded.

"What'd she tell Art about me?"

"She told him to tell you that despite everything she thinks you're 'a real neat guy.' "

Becker said nothing. After a few minutes, Carol said she would see him at the story conference, and walked out of the office.

Becker found that he was surprised but not, in fact, upset. Compared to being, say, the operator of a holistic podiatry clinic or an acolyte of some loony guru, being the social director of a singles apartment in Phoenix didn't seem like such a bad thing for Greta to be doing. At least he wouldn't have to worry about having her try to sell him flowers in an airport.

The telephone rang, and Becker picked it up. "Aren't you coming to the preliminary?" Genine said. Becker said he was, and walked toward Pete Smithers' office. It was customary to invite the section's writer to attend the preliminary story conference for the following week's list—even though, in Becker's case, he would be writing Music rather than Lifestyle the following week. No official notification had come, but Becker had already received a telephone call from Yitzchak Katz suggesting a Music story on a speech by Simchas Golbhelder, the Smetena rebbe, denouncing a Reform rabbi who was said to be composing a rock Kol

Nidre service. Becker decided that he would sit in for a few minutes, then get back to the two-thirds stockings story, which Smithers wanted "livened up a little."

The usual crowd was there—unless an impostor was wearing Smithers' Bass Weejuns. As Becker walked in, they seemed to be discussing a personalized wake-up service in Denver—a service whose operators would whisper sensually in the ear of a lonely spinster or shout crudely at a former army sergeant. Smithers' voice was coming out from behind his desk with instructions for Carol Goodenow.

"And Carol, honey," Smithers said, "make sure in the query you emphasize the Lifestyle angle, so the guy in Denver doesn't try to show off by sending in all this balance sheet crap and Woody decides it's a Business story. The Business section thinks the goddamnned Superbowl is a Business story just because the players get paid."

Carol looked flushed. Becker thought for a moment that Smithers had included some sort of double-entendre in his instructions. Then, in a clear and controlled voice, Carol said, "Pete, in my official capacity as chairperson of the Women Employees Committee, I remind you that under the terms of an agreement reached last March between management and the W. E. C., a memorandum from the managing editor was distributed forbidding editors and writers from addressing female employees by such terms as 'honey' or 'sweetie,' and that you, having been specifically named in the complaint that eventually resulted in the agreement, signed a separate consent agreement promising to cease and desist from such behavior in the future."

"Jesus Christ!" Smithers said. "Jesus H. Christ!" He had snapped up to his crisis position—both feet on the floor, hands on his desk.

"Do you want me to show you the documents in question?" Carol said. Becker was amazed once more at how strong she was at such moments. He thought he might take a chance on asking her to dinner after all. What if she did blush or call him a chauvinist?

There was a long silence. Finally, Smithers said, "I'm sorry. I won't do it again."

"Thank you," Carol said. "We appreciate your cooperation."

"Now, what about this story about people collecting ice-cream scoops?" Smithers asked.

"Sink stoppers," Genine said. "We did ice-cream scoops."

Becker walked out of the story conference and headed for his office, resolved to have another go at the two-thirds stockings story. Leonard Wentzell was sitting at his desk.

"Pal of my youth," Wentzell said, with a clumsy wave. Wentzell was dressed in his usual disarray. He was holding a bag of potato chips, the crumbs of which were visible on Becker's desk.

Becker didn't say anything.

"Some security arrangements you have here these days," Wentzell said. "The gentleman downstairs practically wanted my grandmother's maiden name before he would permit me near the elevator. Fortunately, I happen to be carrying some identity papers that he found rather impressive. Potato chip?" Wentzell held out the sack.

Becker shook his head.

"I acknowledge, Freddy, the obvious fact that I deceived you," Wentzell said. "On the other hand, you have always known me to be deceitful, so it wasn't as if I pretended to be anything I wasn't."

Becker nodded. "How's Mary Jane?" he said.

"Fine, thanks. Just fine. She sends her regards. I think she's just about forgiven you."

"Forgiven me for what?"

"Well, difficult as it may be to believe, there was some coolness when we met again in Washington, even after all these years, because of the unfortunate root beer incident in high school. I thought things might go a bit easier if I told her that you had made a remark about her maracas that I was just adding to—and that you goaded me into throwing the root beer. I thought you probably wouldn't mind having your name used in that way. After all—"

"It's a good cause," Becker said.

"Precisely, comrade of my salad days. A good cause. In return, I will take you to a long, wet lunch and tell you a little tale I think might just lead to the blossoming of your career—perhaps to the editorship of this cockamamie sheet."

"I've got this two-thirds stockings story," Becker said.

"It'll be there when you get back, Freddy," Wentzell said, rising with some difficulty, tossing the empty potato chip bag in the general direction of the wastebasket, and handing Becker his jacket.

"Why not," Becker said, getting into his jacket. They walked out of the office together.

"Is that two-thirds of the way up the leg or two-thirds of the way to the knee?" Wentzell said, as they walked down the hall toward the elevator. "Or what?"

"Two-thirds of the way up the leg," Becker said. "That much we know."